STIR FRY RECIPES

Quick & Easy Gluten Free Low Recipes

(A Stir Fry Cookbook Filled With Delicious Chicken Recipes)

Loren Hang

Published by Sharon Lohan

© **Loren Hang**

All Rights Reserved

Stir Fry Recipes: Quick & Easy Gluten Free Low Recipes (A Stir Fry Cookbook Filled With Delicious Chicken Recipes)

ISBN 978-1-990334-46-7

All rights reserved. No part of this guide may be reproduced in any form without permission in writing from the publisher except in the case of brief quotations embodied in critical articles or reviews.

Legal & Disclaimer

The information contained in this book is not designed to replace or take the place of any form of medicine or professional medical advice. The information in this book has been provided for educational and entertainment purposes only.

The information contained in this book has been compiled from sources deemed reliable, and it is accurate to the best of the Author's knowledge; however, the Author cannot guarantee its accuracy and validity and cannot be held liable for any errors or omissions. Changes are periodically made to this book. You must consult your doctor or get professional medical advice before using any of the suggested remedies, techniques, or information in this book.

Table of contents

Part 1 1
Introduction 2
Sweet And Garlicky Chicken Stir Fry 4
Ramen Stir Fry 6
Maple And Cashew Veggie Stir Fry 8
Veggie Brown Rice Stir Fry 10
Teriyaki Chicken Stir Fry 12
Honey And Garlic Shrimp Stir Fry 14
Ground Turkey Stir Fry 16
Mongolian Beef Stir Fry 18
Simple Beef And Broccoli Stir Fry 20
Chicken Lo Mein 22
Pepper Steak Stir Fry 24
Thai Noodle Stir Fry 26
Egg Roll Stir Fry 28
Sriracha Beef And Cabbage Stir Fry 30
Lemon Chicken Stir Fry 32
Veggie Tofu Stir Fry 34
Shrimp And Zoodle Stir Fry 36
Zucchini, Squash, And Chicken In A Sweet Chili Sauce ... 38
Rainbow Veggie Stir Fry 40
Sugar Snap Pea Pork Stir Fry 42
Okra And Rice Stir Fry 44
Mongolian Vegan Noodle Stir Fry 45
Leftover Turkey Stir Fry 47

Kung Pao Shrimp	49
Cauliflower Rice Veggie Stir Fry	51
Chicken, Mushroom, And Green Bean Stir Fry	53
Tempeh Stir Fry In A Gingery Peanut Sauce	55
Szechuan Chicken Stir Fry	57
Apple Cider Kale Stir Fry	59
Chili Shrimp Noodle Stir Fry	61
Mango Chicken Stir Fry	63
Quinoa And Bok Choy Stir Fry	65
Pork And Holy Basil Stir Fry	67
Coconut And Cashew Chicken Stir Fry	69
Bacon And Sausage Cabbage Stir Fry	71
Bamboo Shoot Pork Stir Fry	73
Steak And Sweet Potato Noodle Stir Fry	75
Udon Noodle And Kimchi Stir Fry	77
Indian Chicken Stir Fry	79
Tomato Beef Stir Fry	81
Conclusion	83
Part 2	84
Introduction	85
Delicious Stir-Fry Recipes	89
Vegetables	90
Ginger And Asparagus Stir-Fry	90
Classic Vegetable Stir-Fry	92
Peppered Brussels Sprouts	93
Garlic And Bitter Melon Stir-Fry	94
Asian Bok Choy Toss	95

Soy Cabbage Stir-Fry	96
Tomato And Egg Stir-Fry	97
Beef	98
Sirloin Stir-Fry	98
Beef And Peas Stir-Fry	100
Garlic And Beef Stir-Fry	102
Beef In Oyster Sauce Stir-Fry	103
Beef And Baby Corn Stir-Fry	104
Beef And Broccoli Stir-Fry	105
Peppered Sesame Beef Stir-Fry	106
Ponzu Sauce Beef Toss	107
Chili Beef Stir-Fry	108
Beef And Cilantro Stir-Fry	109
Pork	110
Peppered Pork Stir-Fry	110
Wansoy Pork Stir-Fry	112
Vietnamese Pork Stir-Fry	113
Pineapple And Pork Stir-Fry	115
Perfect Pork Stir-Fry	116
Peppered Pork And Peas Stir-Fry	118
Pork And Ginger Wok Toss	120
Cauliflower And Ham Stir-Fry	121
Spicy Pork Strips Stir-Fry	122
Peaches And Pork Stir-Fry	124
Chicken	125
Ginger Chicken Stir-Fry	125
Pecan Chicken Stir-Fry	127

Garlic Chicken Asian Toss	128
Orange Chicken Chow Mein	129
Seafood	131
Basil Shrimp Stir-Fry	131
Salt And Pepper Salmon Toss	133
Caribbean Shrimp Stir-Fry	134
Curry Shrimp Stir-Fry	135
Stir Fry Recipes	136
Mushroom & Bell Peppers Stir Fry	136
Broccoli & Bell Pepper Stir Fry	138
Cauliflower Stir Fry	140
Kale Stir Fry	142
Broccoli & Zucchini Stir Fry	144
Spicy Potato Stir Fry	146
Sesame Beef Stir Fry	148
Ginger & Chiles Beef Stir Fry	150
Beef & Orange Stir Fry	152
Beef & Green Beans Stir Fry	154
Beef & Mushroom Stir Fry	156
Ground Beef, Bell Pepper & Cabbage Stir Fry	158
Chicken, Veggies & Fruit Stir Fry	160
Chicken & Tofu Stir Fry	162
Chicken & Mixed Veggies Stir Fry	164
Chicken, Mushrooms & Eggplant Stir Fry	166
Chicken & Bok Choy Stir Fry With Almonds	168
Chicken & Carrot Stir Fry	170
Chicken & Apricot Stir Fry	172

Chicken, Bell Pepper & Pineapple Stir Fry	174
Pork, Apple & Veggies Stir Fry	176
Pork & Cucumbers Stir Fry	178
Pork & Ginger Stir Fry	180
Pork, Snow Peas & Pineapple Stir Fry	182
Pork, Veggies & Peach Stir Fry	184
Garlicky Prawn Stir Fry	186
Shrimp, Asparagus & Pasta Stir Fry	188

Part 1

Introduction

Do you struggle to find the balance between the soy sauce, the rice vinegar, the honey, and the other ingredients you are stirring into your wok? If so, then buying this book will save you from your failed attempts to create that takeout stir fry that you like so much. This book will help you make it even better.

Offering you 40 different ways to prepare a stir fry, whether with meat or not, this is the only cookbook that will show you the true worth of your wok. Delicious and nutritious, the stir fry recipes in this book will not only satisfy your tummy and taste buds, but they will also boost your immune and pack you with feel-good vibes.

Whether on rice or noodles, these amazing delicacies are simple to make, and they can all be mastered by you after the very first attempt.

Jump to the first recipe and see what I am talking about.

Sweet And Garlicky Chicken Stir Fry

Garlic, honey, carrots and broccoli accompany chicken in this delicious and simple-to-make stir fry that is cooked to perfection and fried in a savory sweet sauce that will have you licking your plate in no time.

Serves: 4

- 2 cups Broccoli Florets
- 1 cup sliced Carrots
- ¼ cup Soy Sauce
- 3 tbsp. Honey
- 1 pound Chicken Breasts, cut into cubes
- ¼ cup Chicken Broth
- 2 tsp Cornstarch
- 4 Garlic Cloves, minced
- 2 tsp Cornstarch
- 1 tbsp. plus 1 tsp Oil
- ¼ tsp Salt
- ¼ tsp Pepper

Preparation:
Heat a teaspoon of oil in a pan over medium heat. Add carrots and broccoli. Cook for about 3-4 minutes. Transfer the veggies to a pan and heat the remaining oil in the pan. Add chicken, salt, and pepper, and cook until golden. Add garlic and cook for 30 more seconds. Return the veggies to the pan. In a bowl, whisk together the remaining ingredients. Pour the sauce over and cook for a few minutes, until thickened. Serve and enjoy!

Ramen Stir Fry

Packaged ramen noodles combined with a bunch of veggies in a sweet and flavorful sauce. This noodle dish is ready in only 20 minutes, and is the perfect choice for your Asian dinner nights.

Serves: 4

- 9 ounces packaged Ramen Noodles
- 2 tbsp Sesame Oil
- 2 Chicken Flavor Packets
- 2 ½ cups chopped Veggies (asparagus, carrots, snow peas, celery, broccoli…)
- 1 cup chopped Onion
- 2 tbsp. Olive Oil
- 1/3 cup Hoisin Sauce
- 1 tbsp. granulated Garlic
- 1/3 cup Mr. Yoshida Sauce
- ¾ cup Cold Water

Preparation:
Bring a bowl of water to a boil and then cook the noodles in it for about 2 minutes, or until tender. Drain and set it aside.
In a skillet, heat the olive oil over medium heat. Add onion and cook for 2 minutes.
Add the chopped vegetables and cook for 3 more minutes.
Stir in the ramen and remaining ingredients. Toss to coat everything well.
Cook for 1 minute and serve immediately. Enjoy!

Maple And Cashew Veggie Stir Fry

A sweet sauce with maple syrup, garlic, and ginger, combine the peppers, cauliflower, and broccoli in the most flavorful and delicious way. The cashew topping gives this stir fry a heavenly crunchiness and takes it to the next level.

Serves: 4

- 1 tbsp. Olive Oil
- 1 ½ cups Cauliflower Florets
- 1 ½ cups Broccoli Florets
- ½ cup chopped Red Bell Pepper
- ½ cup Yellow Bell Pepper
- ½ cup Green Bell Pepper
- ½ tsp Salt
- ½ cup chopped Cashews
- 1 Green Onion, sliced

Sauce:

- 3 ½ tsp minced Garlic
- 1 ½ tbsp. Lemon Juice
- 1/3 cup Tamari Sauce
- 3 ½ tbsp. Maple Syrup
- 1 tsp toasted Sesame Oil
- 2 tsp minced Ginger
- 1 tsp Blackstrap Molasses
- 1 tbsp. Arrowroot Powder
- 1/3 cup Water

Preparation:
Heat the olive oil in a wok over the medium heat. Add broccoli and peppers and cook for a couple of minutes, until soft.
Meanwhile, whisk together all of the sauce ingredients in a bowl.
Increase the heat to high and pour the sauce over the veggies.
Bring it to a slow boil, then reduce to simmer, and cook until thickened. Stir in the cashews and green onions. Serve immediately and enjoy!

Veggie Brown Rice Stir Fry

Who needs meat when there is this yummy recipe? Packed with brown rice, red cabbage, broccoli, zucchini, and bell pepper, this stir fry wrapped in irresistible garlicky flavor will blow your mind.

Serves: 4
Ready In: 45 minutes
Ingredients:

- ½ cup chopped Zucchini
- 1 cup chopped red Cabbage
- 1 Bell Pepper, chopped
- ½ Head of Broccoli, broken into Florets
- ½ cup uncooked Brown Rice
- 4 Garlic Cloves, minced
- 2 tbsp. Olive Oil
- Pinch of Cayenne Pepper

- 2 tbsp. Soy Sauce
- 1 tbsp. chopped Parsley

Preparation:
Cook the rice following the package instructions. Add enough water in a wok to cover the veggies. Bring it to a boil and then place the veggies in it. Heat for 2 minutes, then drain and set aside. Wipe the wok clean and heat the oil in it. Add garlic, parsley, and cayenne, and cook for 1 minute, until fragrant. Stir in the rice, veggies, and tamari. Cook for 2 minutes. Serve immediately and enjoy!

Teriyaki Chicken Stir Fry

Teriyaki sauce is the star of this recipe and combined with the most famous Asian ingredients, it creates one marvelous dish that you will not be able to resist.

Serves: 4
Ready In: 30 minutes
Ingredients:

- 2 tbsp. Olive Oil
- 2 tbsp. Soy Sauce
- 2 pounds Frozen Veggie Mix
- 1 pound Chicken Breast, cut into chunks
- 2 tsp grated Ginger
- 2 tsp minced Garlic
- 1 tsp Rice Vinegar
- 1 tbsp. Cornstarch
- 1 tbsp. Water

Preparation:
In a wok, heat the oil over medium heat. Add chicken and cook until golden brown on all sides. Stir in the veggies and cook until soft. In a bowl, whisk together the remaining ingredients. Pour the sauce over the chicken and veggies and cook for 3 minutes, or until thickened. Serve and enjoy!

Honey And Garlic Shrimp Stir Fry

Sweet and garlicky flavored, this stir fry with shrimp, white rice, and broccoli, is better than the Asian takeout you are used to. And the very first bite will convince you in that.

Serves: 4
Ready In: 30 minutes
Ingredients:

- 1 ½ cup cooked White Rice
- 1 ½ cups Broccoli Florets
- 1 pound Shrimp, peeled and deveined
- 1/3 cup Honey
- 1 tbsp. minced Garlic
- 1 tsp minced Ginger
- ¼ cup Soy Sauce
- 2 tsp Olive Oil
- Salt and Pepper, to taste

Preparation:
In a bowl, whisk together the ginger, garlic, soy sauce, and honey. Place the shrimp and the broccoli in a Ziploc bag and pour half of the sauce over. Seal and shake to coat well. Let the mixture sit for 15 minutes. Heat the olive oil in a pan and add the shrimp and broccoli along with the juices. Cook for a minute or two, or until set. Stir in the rice and pour the remaining marinade over. Cook until cooked through. Serve and enjoy!

Ground Turkey Stir Fry

This Thai-inspired ground turkey stir fry with peppers and basil in a sweet and tangy sauce is not only filling and delicious but it is also one of those meals that you simply devour.

Serves: 6
Ready In: 20 minutes
Ingredients:

- 1 Onion, chopped
- 1 ½ cups Basil Leaves
- 1 ½ pounds ground Turkey
- 1 Red Bell Pepper, cut into strips
- 1 tsp Avocado Oil
- 2 tsp minced Garlic

Sauce:

- 1 tbsp. Agave Nectar
- 1 tbsp. Fish Sauce
- 1 tbsp. Soy Sauce
- 2 tbsp. fresh Lime Juice
- 1 tbsp. Sriracha Sauce

Preparation:
Whisk together all of the sauce ingredients in a bowl. Set aside.
Heat the oil in a wok and cook the onion and peppers until soft.
Add garlic and cook for 30 seconds or so, or just until fragrant.
Add turkey and cook until it becomes browned. Stir in the basil and cook until it becomes wilted. Pour the sauce over and cook for 2 minutes. Serve immediately and enjoy!

Mongolian Beef Stir Fry

Peppers, broccoli, water chestnut and flank steak star in this hoisin sauce delicacy that will water your mouth the seconds you start cooking. Rich and flavorful, this Mongolian stir fry satisfies all tastes.

Serves: 4
Ready In: 30 minutes
Ingredients:

- 1 pound Flank Steak, cut into strips
- 2 tbsp. Oil
- 3 tbsp. Cornstarch
- 1 cup chopped Peppers
- ½ cup sliced Water Chestnuts
- 3 Green Onions, chopped
- 1 Broccoli Head, cut into florets

Sauce:

- 2 tbsp. Rice Vinegar
- 1/3 cup Hoisin Sauce
- 2 tsp minced Garlic
- ½ tsp grated Ginger
- 1/3 cup Soy Sauce
- 2 tbsp. Brown Sugar
- ½ cup Water
- ½ tsp Chili Paste

Preparation:
Toss the beef with cornstarch and heat the oil in a pan over medium heat.
Add beef and cook until browned on all sides. Transfer to a plate.
Add the veggies and cook until soft, for a couple of minutes.
Meanwhile, whisk the sauce ingredients together in a bowl.
Pour the sauce over the veggies and add the beef to the pan. Stir to combine and cook for a few minutes, or until the sauce thickens.

Simple Beef And Broccoli Stir Fry

If you are looking for a simple stir fry recipe with beef, then this is probably the most basic way to prepare it. Beef and broccoli in a simple sweet sauce with brown sugar and soy sauce.

Serves: 4
Ready In: 25 minutes
Ingredients:

- 1 pound Round Steak
- 2 tbsp. Vegetable Oil
- 4 cups Broccoli Florets
- ½ cup plus 2 tbsp. Water
- 3 tbsp. Cornstarch
- 1 Onion, sliced
- 2 tbsp. Brown Sugar
- 1 tsp ground Ginger
- 1/3 cup Soy Sauce
- ½ tsp Garlic Powder

Preparation:
Whisk together 2 tbsp. water, 2 tbsp. cornstarch, and the garlic powder, in a bowl. Add the beef and toss to coat it well. Heat half of the oil in a wok over the medium heat. Add beef and cook until browned on all sides. Transfer to a plate. Heat the remaining oil and cook the onion and broccoli until soft. Return the beef to the pan. In a bowl, whisk together the remaining ingredients. Pour the sauce over the beef and veggies. Cook for 2 more minutes, or until thickened.

Chicken Lo Mein

Chicken lo Mein is one of the most famous stir fry recipes, and if you are a fan of the Asian takeout meals, then this recipe is just what you need to make for dinner to satisfy your taste buds.

Serves: 6
Ready In: 30 minutes
Ingredients:

- 2 Chicken Breasts, cut into chunks
- 4 tbsp. Olive Oil
- 1 cup Chinese Cabbage, shredded
- 2 tbsp. Soy Sauce
- 2 cups sliced Shitake Mushrooms
- 1 Onion, chopped
- 1 cup grated Carrots
- 2 tap minced Garlic

- 1 tsp minced Ginger
- 16 ounces Ramen Noodles
- 2 Spring Onions, chopped

Sauce:

- 1 tbsp. Oyster Sauce
- 1 tsp Hoisin Sauce
- 1 tbsp. Brown Sugar
- 2 tbsp. Soy Sauce
- 1 tsp Pepper
- 2 tbsp. Dark Soy Sauce
- 1 tsp Sesame Oil

Preparation:
Cook the noodles according the package instructions. Drain and place in a bowl.
Toss the chicken with ginger, 2 tbsp. soy sauce, and ginger.
Use a wok to heat half of the olive oil and add the chicken.
Cook until golden on all sides, for about 5 minutes. Transfer to a plate.
Heat the rest oil in the wok. Add the veggies, except the green onions, and cook for a few more minutes, until soft.
Move the chicken back to the wok.
Meanwhile, whisk together the sauce ingredients in a bowl. Pour the mixture over the chicken and veggies. Stir to combine and cook for 2 minutes.

Serve over noodles and sprinkle with green onions. Serve and enjoy!

Pepper Steak Stir Fry

Peppers, steak, green onions, ginger, and soy sauce are the main ingredients in this Chinese stir fry that is excellent served on rice. A colorful dish that is packed with rich flavors.

Serves: 4
Ready In: 30 minutes
Ingredients:

- 1 pound Sirloin Steak, cut into strips
- 1 ½ Bell Peppers (different colors), sliced
- 2 Green Onions, sliced
- 2 tbsp. minced Ginger
- 1 ½ tsp minced Garlic
- 2 tbsp. Olive Oil

Marinade:

- ¼ cup Soy Sauce
- 1 tbsp. Cornstarch
- 1/3 cup Water
- Pinch of Pepper
- 2 tbsp. Rice Wine Vinegar

Preparation:

Whisk the marinade ingredients in a bowl. Place the steak in a Ziploc bag and pour the marinade over.

Seal the bag and shake to coat well. Let it marinate for 15 minutes.

Heat half of the oil in a wok. Add the white parts of the peppers and onions, and cook until softened.

Add ginger and garlic and cook for an additional minute. Transfer to a plate.

Heat the remaining oil and add the steak, without the marinade.

Cook until the steak is browned on all sides. Return the veggies to the wok along with the green parts of the onions.

Pour the marinade over and cook for 2 more minutes. Serve and enjoy!

Thai Noodle Stir Fry

Originally called Pad See Ew, this popular Thai street food is consisting of stir fried noodles in a salty and sour, but very balanced sauce. Combined with chicken and Chinese broccoli, this is super enjoyable.

Serves: 4
Ready In: 30 minutes
Ingredients:

- 6 ounces Wide Rice Noodles
- 2 tbsp. Peanut Oil
- 2 Garlic Cloves, minced
- 1 cup chopped Chicken Thighs
- 1 Egg
- 4 cups Chinese Broccoli, leaves separated and chopped

Sauce:

- 2 tbsp. Dark Soy Sauce
- 2 tsp White Vinegar
- 2 tbsp Oyster Sauce
- 2 tbsp Water
- 2 tsp Sugar
- 2 tsp Regular Soy Sauce

Preparation:
Cook the noodles as stated on the package. Drain and place in a bowl. Heat the oil in a wok and add garlic. Cook for 1 minute until fragrant. Add chicken and the stems of the Chinese Broccoli. Cook until the chicken turns golden on all sides. Move them to the side of the pan and add the egg. Scramble and cook until set. Add the noodles and the leaves of the broccoli. Whisk all of the sauce ingredients in a bowl and pour the sauce over. Cook until the leaves become wilted. Serve immediately and enjoy!

Egg Roll Stir Fry

If you love eating egg rolls, then you will definitely fall in love with this recipe. Your favorite egg roll filling as a full stir fry meal. Serve over rice if you want to.

Serves: 4
Ready In: 20 minutes
Ingredients:

- 1 pound ground Pork
- 1 Onion, diced
- 1 tbsp. Oil
- 1 small Cabbage Head, sliced
- 3 Carrots, sliced
- 2 tbsp. Sesame Oil
- 4 Garlic Cloves, minced
- ¼ cup Soy Sauce
- ½ tsp Pepper
- 1 tbsp. grated Ginger

Preparation:
Heat the oil in a pan over medium heat.

Cook the onions and pork until the pork becomes browned.

Add the carrots and cabbage and cook for 3 more minutes.

Meanwhile whisk together the ginger, soy sauce, garlic, pepper, and sesame oil, in a bowl. Pour the mixture over.

Cook for a few more minutes. Serve and enjoy!

Sriracha Beef And Cabbage Stir Fry

Spiced up with some sriracha and wrapped up beautifully in a sweet and salty sauce, this stir fry with beef and cabbage has just what you are looking for in Asian takeout meals.

Serves: 4
Ready In: 30 minutes
Ingredients:

- ½ Green Cabbage, thinly sliced
- 2 Carrots, shredded
- 3 Green Onions, chopped
- ½ pound ground Beef
- 1 tbsp. grated Ginger
- 1 tbsp. toasted Sesame Oil
- 2 tbsp. Soy Sauce
- 2 tbsp. Sriracha
- ½ tbsp. Olive Oil

- 1 tsp minced Garlic
- ½ tbsp. Brown Sugar

Preparation:
In a bowl, whisk together the soy sauce, brown sugar, half of sriracha, and sesame oil. Set aside.
Heat the oil in a wok and add the beef, ginger, and garlic.
Cook until the beef is browned.
Add the veggies and cook for a few more minutes, until the cabbage reaches your desired consistency.
Pour the sauce over and cook for a few more minutes.
Serve drizzled with the remaining Sriracha. Enjoy!

Lemon Chicken Stir Fry

Packed with veggies, rich in amazing flavors, and most importantly, healthy, this lemon chicken stir fry is just what you need to boost your immune during those cold winter days. Serve over brown rice for a full meal.

Serves: 4
Ready In: 22 minutes
Ingredients:

- 1 pound Chicken Breasts, cut into strips
- ½ Onion, chopped
- 1 pound Zucchini, chopped
- 6 ounces Mushrooms, sliced
- 2 tsp Sesame Oil

Sauce:

- 1 cup Chicken Broth
- ½ tbsp. Sesame Oil
- 1 tbsp. Lemon Juice
- Zest of ½ Lemon
- ½ tbsp. Sesame Oil
- ½ tsp Fish Sauce
- 1 tbsp. Soy Sauce
- 2 Garlic Cloves, minced
- 1 ½ tbsp. Cornstarch

Preparation:
Whisk together all of the sauce ingredients in a bowl. Set it aside. Heat a wok over high heat and add half of the oil. Cook the chicken for 5 minutes, or until it is golden on all sides. Then transfer to a plate. Heat the remaining oil and add the veggies. Cook until they become soft. Return the chicken to the pan and pour the sauce over. Cook for a few minutes. Serve and enjoy!

Veggie Tofu Stir Fry

Peppers and broccoli with tofu in a red curry sauce is all you need for dinner. Unique in flavor and fragrant and rich in the most amazing taste, this stir fry will be the favorite one for every vegetarian.

Serves: 4
Ready In: 20 minutes
Ingredients:

- 1 pound Tofu, cubed
- 1 Red Bell Pepper, sliced
- 1 Yellow Bell Pepper, sliced
- 1 Green Bell Pepper, sliced
- 1 tbsp. grated Ginger
- 12 ounces Broccoli Florets
- 3 tbsp. Sesame Oil
- 3 tbsp. Water
- 1 ½ tsp Arrowroot

- 2 tbsp Red Curry Paste
- 1/3 cup Soy Sauce

Preparation:

In a bowl, whisk together the water, arrowroot, soy sauce, and red curry paste. Set aside. Heat the sesame oil in a wok over the medium heat. Add tofu and cook for about 3 minutes. Then stir in the peppers and ginger and cook until soft, about 5 minutes. Add broccoli florets and cook for 2 minutes. Pour the sauce over and cook until it thickens, a couple of minutes.

Shrimp And Zoodle Stir Fry

Shrimp, zoodles, snap peas, carrots, bell pepper, and onions give this stir fry a delectable and unique flavor that it's easy to resist. Serve this recipe as it is and enjoy.

Serves: 4
Ready In: 25 minutes
Ingredients:

- 1 pound Shrimp, peeled and deveined
- 2/3 cup sliced Red Onions
- 1 cup Snap Peas
- 2 Zucchinis, spiralized into noodles
- 2 tsp Cornstarch
- 1 Bell Pepper, sliced
- ½ cup shredded Carrots
- 1 tsp minced Ginger
- ½ cup Chicken Broth
- 1 tbsp. Soy Sauce

- ¼ cup Hoisin Sauce
- 1 tbsp. minced Garlic
- 3 tbsp. Olive Oil

Preparation:
Whisk the cornstarch, hoisin sauce, soy sauce, and broth, in a bowl. Set aside. Heat 2 tbsp. of the oil in a wok over the medium heat. Add garlic and ginger and cook for 1 minute. Add shrimp and cook on all sides, for about 3 minutes in total. Transfer to a bowl. Heat the remaining oil and add onions and peppers. Cook until soft and stir in the carrots and snap peas. Cook for additional 3 minutes. Pour the sauce over and cook for a couple of minutes, or until thickened. Stir in the shrimp and noodles, and cook for 1 minute.

Zucchini, Squash, And Chicken In A Sweet Chili Sauce

A sweet and chili stir fry with chicken, squash, and zucchini. The rice wine vinegar makes all the difference so be sure not to leave it out or substitute with another ingredient.

Serves: 6
Ready In: 30 minutes
Ingredients:

- 4 tbsp. Olive Oil
- 2 small Zucchini, chopped
- 2 small Squashes, chopped
- 3 Chicken Breasts, chopped
- 1 Onion, chopped
- Salt and Pepper, to taste

Sauce:

- 1 tbsp. Cold Water
- ¾ cup Sweet and Chili Sauce
- 2 tbsp. Honey
- 3 tbsp Soy Sauce
- 1 tbsp. Cornstarch
- 1 tbsp. Rice Wine Vinegar

Preparation:

Heat half of the oil in a wok on the medium heat. Add chicken, season with some pepper and salt, and cook until golden on all sides. Transfer to a plate. Heat the remaining oil and sauté the onions for 2 minutes.

Add squash and zucchini and cook for few more minutes until tender, but not soggy. Meanwhile, whisk together the sauce ingredients, in a bowl.

Pour over the vegggies and stir in the chicken. Cook until the sauce thickens and serve.

Rainbow Veggie Stir Fry

Different veggie colors = different vitamins. And this stir fry is packed with them all. Prepare with your favorite sauce and serve over rice or noodles. Absolutely yummy!

Serves: 2
Ready In: 20 minutes
Ingredients:

- ¼ Red Cabbage, chopped
- 1 Large Red Bell Pepper, chopped
- ½ Broccoli Head, broken into florets
- 2 Carrots, shredded
- ½ Yellow Bell Pepper, chopped
- 1 tbsp. Lime Juice
- 2 tbsp. Oil
- 1 cup favorite Sauce (I suggest Asian Peanut Sauce)

Preparation:
Heat half of the oil in a medium heat in a wok. Add onion and garlic and cook for 1 minute. Add peppers and continue cooking for another 3 minutes.
Add the remaining oil and stir in the rest of the ingredients.
Cook until the veggies are tender. Pour the sauce over and cook for 2 more minutes. Serve over rice and noodles. Enjoy!

Sugar Snap Pea Pork Stir Fry

This stir fry with pork loin, sugar snap peas, carrots, peppers, and rice, is a real crowd pleaser. Prepared in a simple sweet and tangy sauce, this stir fry is the ultimate Chinese dinner.

Serves: 4
Ready In: 30 minutes
Ingredients:

- 1 pound Boneless Pork Loin, chopped
- 1 tbsp. Cornstarch
- 1 tbsp. Oyster Sauce
- 3 tbsp. Soy Sauce
- 1 tbsp. Lime Juice
- 3 tbsp. Canola Oil
- 1 tbsp. minced Ginger
- 3 Scallions, chopped
- 2 Carrots, sliced
- 1 tbsp. chopped Cilantro

- 2 tsp minced Garlic
- 1 Red Bell Pepper, cut into strips
- 8 ounces Sugar Snap Peas
- 2 cups cooked White Rice

Preparation:

Place the pork, cornstarch and 1 tbsp. soy sauce, in a bowl. Mix to coat well.
In another bowl, whisk together the rest of the soy sauce, lime juice, and oyster sauce, and set aside.
Heat 2 tbsp. of oil in wok and add the pork. Cook until the pork is browned on all sides. Transfer to a plate.
Heat the remaining oil and add the other fragrant ingredients (ginger, scallion, garlic). Cook for only one minute.
Add carrots and peppers and cook for 2 more minutes.
Stir in the sugar snap peas and cook for additional 2-3 minutes.
Add the pork and pour the sauce over. Stir in the rice.
Cook for a minute or two more until cooked through and combined. Serve immediately and enjoy!

Okra And Rice Stir Fry

Made with only ingredients and ready in just 10 minutes, this stir fry with okra and cooked rice is the definition of a quick and easy dinner.

Serves: 2
Ready In: 10 minutes
Ingredients:

- 2 dried Chili Peppers
- 1 ½ cups cooked White Rice
- 7 ounces Okra, chopped
- 2 tbsp. Soy Sauce
- 1 tsp Sichuan Peppercorn

Preparation:

Grease your wok well with cooking spray and heat over medium heat. Add the Sichuan peppercorn and cook for a minute, until it becomes dark and fragrant. Break the chili peppers into the wok. Add the okra and cook for 1 minute. Add half of soy sauce and cook the mixture for 3 minutes.

Stir in the cooked rice and the remaining soy sauce and cook for another minute or so. Serve and enjoy!

Mongolian Vegan Noodle Stir Fry

If you are a vegan and a busy worker, you will highly appreciate this quick and easy dish. Made with purple cabbage, kale, bell pepper and baby corn, this nutrient-pack stir fry is a good immune booster.

Serves: 6

- 9 Noodles of Choice
- 1 cup shredded Purple Cabbage
- 1 Bell Pepper, sliced
- 2 cups chopped Kale
- ½ cup Baby Corn
- 2 tbsp. Sugar
- 3 tsp Red Chilly Sauce
- 1 tbsp. plus 2 tsp Oil
- 3 tbsp. plus 1 tsp Dark Soy Sauce
- 2 tbsp. grated Ginger

- 1 tbsp. Sesame Oil
- 1 tsp Pepper

Preparation:

Cook the noodles following the package instructions. Drain and toss with 1 tsp soy sauce, 2 tsp oil, and 1 tsp chili sauce. Set aside.
In a bowl, whisk together the seasonings, sauces, and sugar.
Heat the oil in a wok over the medium heat. Add ginger and cook for 30-35 seconds. Add the vegies and cook until they are tender. Stir in the noodles and pour the sauce over. Cook for about 2 minutes, or until well combined and cooked through. Serve immediately and enjoy!

Leftover Turkey Stir Fry

When you don't know what to do with your leftover turkey, here is a solution – make this delightful stir fry. Ready in just 20 minutes. This veggie and turkey stir fry in a fragrant sauce will please everyone.

Serves: 4

- 1 pound leftover Turkey Meat, shredded
- 1 pound frozen Veggie Mix (broccoli, carrots, peas, etc.)
- 1 tbsp. Rice Vinegar
- 1 Onion, chopped
- 1 tbsp. minced Ginger
- 1 tbsp. minced Garlic
- 2 tsp Sesame Oil
- 3 tbsp. Soy Sauce
- 1 tbsp. Honey
- 1 tsp Cornstarch
- 2 tbsp. Avocado Oil

Preparation:
Place the veggies in a microwave safe bowl and add a splash of water. Microwave for 3-4 minutes, or until tender. In a bowl, whisk together the honey, rice vinegar, soy sauce, and cornstarch. Set aside. Heat the avocado oil in a wok over the medium heat. Add onions and cook for 3 minutes, or as long as it needs for them to become soft. Add the garlic and then stir the ginger into the well as well. Cook for 30 seconds. Stir in the veggies and turkey. Pour the sauce over and cook until it thickens, 2-3 minutes. Serve and enjoy!

Kung Pao Shrimp

Shrimp, veggies, and peanuts are the stars of this classic Asian dish. If you love this spicy and sweet take out, then you will be amazed to know that you can easily make one in your own kitchen.

Serves: 4
Ready In: 20 minutes
Ingredients:

- ½ Red Bell Pepper, cut into strips
- ½ Green Bell Pepper, cut into strips
- 1 pound large Shrimp, peeled and deveined
- 1 tbsp. Oil
- ½ Yellow Onion, chopped
- 1 tsp minced Garlic
- 4 dried Red Chilies, seeded and halved
- ½ cup unsalted Peanuts

Sauce:

- 2 tsp Cornstarch
- 1 tbsp. Hoisin Sauce
- 2 tsp Sugar
- 2 tbsp. Water
- 2 tbsp. Soy Sauce
- 2 tsp Sesame Oil

Preparation:

Heat the oil in wok over the medium heat. Add onion and cook for 3 minutes. Add the peppers and cook for additional 2-3 minutes. Stir in the garlic and cook only for 30 seconds. Add shrimp and cook on all sides for about 3 minutes in total. Meanwhile, whisk together all of the sauce ingredients in a bowl. Pour the sauce over. Cook until it thickens, about 2-3 minutes. Serve immediately and enjoy!

Cauliflower Rice Veggie Stir Fry

Light and packed with veggies, this nutritious stir fry in a finger-licking sweet, tangy, and gingery sauce will be your new favorite dish. Throw in some marinated tofu for extra protein if you want to.

Serves: 4
Ready In: 40 minutes
Ingredients:

- 4 cups Cauliflower Rice (ground in a food processor)
- ½ cup Peas
- 1 cup grated Carrots
- 1 Onion, chopped
- 3 Garlic Cloves, minced
- 1 cup Broccoli Florets
- ¼ cup Soy Sauce
- 1 ½ tbsp. Honey
- 1 tsp Red Pepper Flakes

- 1/2 tsp Ginger Powder
- ¼ cup Water

Preparation:
Whisk together all of the ingredients except the veggies, in a bowl.
Grease a wok with cooking spray.
Add the onion and cook for a few minutes or until soft.
Add the remaining veggies, except the cauliflower rice, and cook for 5 minutes.
Stir in the rice and cook for additional 5 minutes. Pour the sauce over and cook until thickened.

Chicken, Mushroom, And Green Bean Stir Fry

Cremini mushrooms and green beans accompany chicken for this lovely stir fry rich in delightful garlicky and gingery sauce. Serve over white rice an enjoy.

Serves: 4
Ready In: 30 minutes
Ingredients:

- 1 pound Chicken Breasts, chopped
- 30 French Green Beans, halved
- 2 tbsp. Canola Oil
- ¼ cup Cornstarch
- 1 tbsp. Sesame Oil
- 2 tsp minced Ginger
- 1 tsp minced Garlic
- ¼ cup Cornstarch
- ¼ cup Soy Sauce

Preparation:

Heat the sesame oil and canola oil in a wok over the medium heat.

Add chicken and cook until it becomes golden on all sides. Transfer to a plate.

Add the mushrooms and cook for 3 minutes. Stir in green beans and cook for 3 minutes. Stir in garlic and ginger and cook for additional 30 seconds.

Return the chicken and pour the sauce over. Cook for 2 more minutes.

Tempeh Stir Fry In A Gingery Peanut Sauce

Rich and creamy in texture thanks to the peanut butter, this vegan stir fry with marinated tempeh and a bunch of veggies is served over white rice for a filling and delicious dinner.

Serves: 4
Ready In: 50 minutes
Ingredients:

- 1 cup shredded Carrots
- 1 cup chopped Kale
- 1 cup shredded Red Cabbage
- 2 cups White Rice

Tempeh:

- 8 ounces Organic Tempeh
- ¼ cup Water
- 1 tsp grated Ginger

- ¼ cup Soy Sauce
- 1 Garlic Clove, minced

Sauce:

- ¾ cup Peanut Butter
- 1 Garlic Clove, minced
- ¼ cup Water
- ¼ cup Soy Sauce
- 1 tsp grated Ginger
- 1 tbsp. Sesame Oil

Preparation:

Chop the tempeh and place in the microwave for a few minutes.

Place in a bowl and stir in the marinade ingredients. Let marinate for 30 minutes. Preheat the oven for 350 degrees F. Arrange the tempeh chunks on a lined baking sheet and bake for 15 minutes, turning once. Meanwhile, cook the rice according the package instructions.

Whisk together all of the ingredients for the sauce. Grease a wok with cooking spray and cook the veggies for a few minutes, until soft. Add the tempeh and pour the sauce over. Cook for a few minutes, or until thickened.

Szechuan Chicken Stir Fry

Chili paste and a bunch of colorful vegetables give this Szechuan chicken stir fry a delicious and spicy taste. Easy to make, delightful, and super nutritious, this recipe is a real keeper.

Serves: 4
Ready In: 25 minutes
Ingredients:

- 1 Egg, whisked
- 1 Onion, julienned
- ½ pound Chicken Breasts, chopped
- 2 tsp minced Garlic
- ½ Red Bell Pepper, chopped
- 1 tsp grated Ginger
- 2 tbsp. Vegetable Oil
- 2 tsp Cornstarch
- 5 Shitake Mushrooms, sliced
- ½ Green Bell Pepper, chopped

Sauce:

- ¼ cup Chicken Stock
- 1 tbsp. Spicy Chili Crisp
- 1 tbsp. Chile Paste
- 1 tsp Cornstarch
- 1 ½ tbsp. Soy Sauce
- ½ tbsp. Rice Vinegar

Preparation:

Combine the chicken, egg, and cornstarch in a bowl and let marinate for 5 minutes.
In another bowl, whisk together all of the remaining ingredients.
Heat half of the oil in a pan and add chicken. Cook until it becomes golden on all sides. Transfer to a plate.
Heat the remaining oil and add the veggies. Cook for a few minutes, until soft.
Add chicken and pour the sauce over. Cook for a few more minutes, until everything is well coated and the sauce is thickened.

Apple Cider Kale Stir Fry

Kale, veggies, and apple combined in a delicious apple cider sauce and stir fried to perfection, make one super satisfying entrée. Sparkling wine is probably the best accompaniment.

Serves: 4
Ready In: 40 minutes
Ingredients:

- 1 Bunch of Kale, chopped
- ¼ Cabbage, sliced
- 1 Green Apple, sliced
- 2 Carrots, spiralized or grated
- 1 Onion, minced
- 1 Green Apple, thinly sliced
- 1 tbsp. Olive Oil
- ½ block Extra Firm Tofu, cubed

Sauce:

- 2 tbsp. Spy Sauce
- 1 cup Apple Cider
- 1 tbsp Apple Cider Vinegar

Preparation:

First, make the sauce. Pour the apple cider in a saucepan over medium heat and let simmer for 20 minutes or so, until it is reduced to about a quarter of a cup. Stir in the vinegar and soy sauce. Add the tofu and marinate until ready to cook. Heat the oil in a pan over medium heat. Add the minced onion and cook for 2 minutes. Add cabbage and cook for 3 minutes. Stir in the kale and carrots. Cover the pan and cook until the kale is wilted. Add tofu along with the marinade. Stir in the apples and serve.

Chili Shrimp Noodle Stir Fry

If you have ever been to Bangkok then you know how absolutely amazing their street food is. This recipe taste just like that. A noodle and shrimp stir fry that will blow your mind.

Serves: 4
Ready In: 15 minutes
Ingredients:

- 1 tbsp. Canola Oil
- 16 Shrimp, peeled and deveined
- 2 Thai Chilies
- 2 tbsp Fish Sauce
- 2 tbsp Dark Soy Sauce
- 1 Egg, whisked
- 1 Tomato, chopped
- 2 tsp chopped Kaffir Lime Leaves
- 2 tsp minced Garlic
- 8 ounces dried Rice Noodles

Preparation:

Cook the noodles according to the package instructions. Drain and set aside.
Heat the oil in a wok and add garlic. Cook for 30 seconds.
Add shrimp and cook until they become opaque. About 3 minutes.
Add the egg and stir in a couple of seconds until set.
Stir in the remaining ingredients and cook until the sauce becomes bubbling.
Add the rice noodles and stir to coat well. Serve immediately.

Mango Chicken Stir Fry

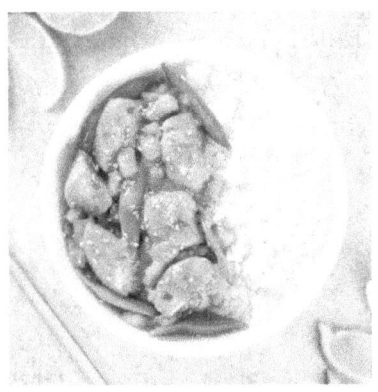

Chicken, bell pepper, and mango in a sweet and slightly chili mango sauce for the most incredible dinner ever. Serve over brown rice for a full meal. You can add some ginger for another fragrant hint.

Serves: 4
Ready In: 30 minutes

Ingredients:

- 3 Chicken Breasts, chopped
- 1 Red Bell Pepper, chopped
- 1 Mango, peeled and sliced
- 1 tsp minced Garlic
- 1 tsp White Vinegar
- ½ tsp Chili Flakes
- 1 ¼ cups Mango Chutney

Preparation:
Spray a pan with cooking spray and heat it over medium heat.

Add chicken and cook until it is golden on all sides. Add peppers and cook for 3 minutes, or until soft. Stir in the remaining ingredients, except the mango, and cook until the sauce begins to bubble. Add the mango slices at this point. Serve over rice.

Quinoa And Bok Choy Stir Fry

Sweet and tangy at the same time, this stir fried made with quinoa, bok choy, peppers, mushrooms, and asparagus is the perfect vegetarian dinner. If you are a meat lover, know that some ground meat can be the perfect addition to this recipe.

Serves: 2
Ready In: 20 minutes
Ingredients:

- 1 cup sliced Mushrooms
- 5 Asparagus Spears, chopped
- ½ cup cooked Quinoa
- 1 tbsp Vegetable Oil
- 1 cup sliced Bell Pepppers
- 1 Head Bok Choy, sliced
- 1 ½ tsp minced Ginger
- 2 tbsp. toasted Sesame Seeds

Sauce:

- ½ tbsp. Lime Juice
- 5 tbsp. Soy Sauce
- 1 ¾ tsp Cornstarch
- ½ tbsp Sesame Oil
- 1 ½ tsp Honey

Preparation:
Heat the oil in a wok over the medium heat. Add the peppers, asparagus, mushrooms, bok choy, and ginger. Cook for about 5 minutes. Meanwhile, whisk together the sauce ingredients, in a bowl.
Pour the sauce over the veggies. Stir and cook until thickened. Stir in quinoa and sesame seeds before serving. Enjoy!

Pork And Holy Basil Stir Fry

The holy basil in this recipe gives the pork a very unique almost licorice-like taste that is very addictive. The Holland chilies wrap this up beautifully. A definite must try!

Serves: 4
Ready In: 30 minutes
Ingredients:

- 2 Shallots, chopped
- 1 tsp Sugar
- 1 pound ground Pork
- 1/3 cup Chicken Broth
- 1 tbsp. Soy Sauce
- 7 Garlic Cloves, minced
- 3 Holland Chilies, thinly sliced
- 1 tbsp. Fish Sauce
- 2 tsp Oyster Sauce
- 1 ½ cups Holy Basil

Preparation:

Heat the oil in a wok over the medium heat. Add shallots and garlic. Cook for about 3 minutes. Stir the chilies in and cook for one more minute. Add pork and cook until browned. Stir in the sugar and sauces and cook for 2 more minutes.

Add the holy basil and cook until wilted. Serve on rice. Enjoy!

Coconut And Cashew Chicken Stir Fry

Light stir fry with chicken, peas in a coconut and honey sauce with a crunchy cashew topping. Does it get better than that? Serve over cooked white rice, sprinkle with extra chopped green onions, and enjoy.

Serves: 4
Ready In: 30 minutes
Ingredients:

- 1 pound Chicken Breast, chopped
- 2 tsp minced Garlic
- 1 cup Snow Peas
- ½ Onion, chopped
- 1 Red Bell Pepper, chopped
- 1 tsp grated Ginger
- ½ cup Cornstarch
- ¼ tsp Garlic Powder
- ¼ tsp Ginger Powder
- ½ tsp Salt

- ¼ cup Coconut Flakes
- 1 cup Cashews

Sauce:

- ½ cup Honey
- 3 tbsp. Apple Cider Vinegar
- 2 tsp Sriracha
- ½ cup Coconut Milk
- 2 tsp Cornstarch
- 2 tbsp Soy Sauce
- Salt and Pepper, to taste

Preparation:

Whisk together the sauce ingredients and set the mixture aside. Coat the chicken with ginger powder, garlic powder, cornstarch and salt. Grease a wok with some cooking spray and cook the chicken until golden; Transfer to a plate. Add onions and pepper and cook for 3 minutes. Add snow peas and chicken to the pan. Pour the sauce over. Cook for a few minutes, or until thickened. Serve topped with coconut flakes and cashews. Enjoy!

Bacon And Sausage Cabbage Stir Fry

Who says that stir fry has to be Asian? Try this sausage and bacon stir fry with cabbage and peppers, and see what I am talking about. Meaty and rich in flavors, this recipe surely satisfies.

Serves: 4
Ready In: 30 minutes
Ingredients:

- 1 ½ tbsp. Canola Oil
- 4 slices Bacon
- 1 Onion, chopped
- 1 pound Kielbasa Sausage, sliced
- 2 tsp minced Garlic
- 1 Red Bell Pepper, sliced
- 1 Cabbage Head, sliced
- Salt and Pepper, to taste

Preparation:
Cook the bacon in a wok over high heat, until crispy. Transfer to a plate.

Add ½ tbsp. oil and kielbasa and cook it until it becomes browned on all sides. Transfer the kielbasa to the plate. Add the remaining oil and onion and peppers. Cook until the veggies become soft, about 3 minutes. Add garlic and cook for another minute. Stir in the cabbage and cook for 3 minutes. Add kielbasa and crumble the bacon over. Season with salt and pepper and serve. Enjoy!

Bamboo Shoot Pork Stir Fry

Bamboo shoots in a stir fry? Now that is what I call the ultimate Asian dish. So, easy and simple to make, and yet so rich in flavor, this dish will keep your family coming back for more.

Serves: 4
Ready In: 30 minutes
Ingredients:

- 3 Thai Chili Peppers, chopped
- 1 cup Jasmine Rice
- 2 Green Onions, chopped
- 2 cups Bamboo Shoots, cut into strips
- 3 Kaffir Lime Leaves, sliced
- 1 cup ground Pork
- 1 tbsp Oyster Sauce
- 2 tbsp. Thin Soy Sauce
- 3 Garlic Cloves, minced

Preparation:
Cook the rice following the package instructions.

Grease a wok with cooking spray over medium heat. Add chilies and garlic and cook for about a minute. Add the pork and cook it until it becomes browned. Stir in the bamboo shoots and the oyster sauce. After a minute, add the lime leaves and onions and cook for 2 more minutes. Stir in the soy sauce and the cooked rice. Serve and enjoy!

Steak And Sweet Potato Noodle Stir Fry

Steak and sweet potato noodles in a soy sauce and gingery sauce and with sesame seeds. This recipe is the best definition of an Asian Stir Fry.

Serves: 2
Ready In: 30 minutes
Ingredients:

- 1 cup Sweet Potato Noodles
- ½ pound Flank Steak, cut into strips
- 1 Bell Pepper, cut into strips
- 2 tbsp. Olive Oil
- ¼ Onion, chopped
- 2 tsp Garlic, minced
- 1/3 cup Soy Sauce
- 1 tbsp. Honey
- 1 tsp Sesame Oil
- ¼ cup Chicken Broth

- 1 tsp grated Ginger
- 1 tsp Vinegar
- 2 tbsp. Sesame Seeds

Preparation:
Heat half of the oil in a pan and add the sweet potato noodles.
Cook for a few minutes, on all sides. Transfer to a plate.
Heat the remaining oil and add the onion and peppers.
Cook for 2 minutes and add the garlic.
After 30 seconds, add the steak and cook until it becomes browned on all sides.
Add the sweet potato noodles and cook everything together for another minute.
Meanwhile, whisk together the honey, soy sauce, ginger, broth, and sesame oil.
Pour the sauce over and cook for a few minutes, until it thickens.
Serve topped with sesame seeds. Enjoy!

Udon Noodle And Kimchi Stir Fry

Ready in just 15 minutes, this stir fry is the ultimate easy meal to prepare in a jiffy on those busy weeknights. Prepare in a spicy and super delicious Korean sauce, this stir fry is just addictive.

Serves: 2
Ready In: 15 minutes
Ingredients:

- 2 packs of Udon Noodles
- 1 cup Kimchi
- ¼ Onion, sliced
- 4 slices Bacon
- 1 Green Onion, sliced
- 1 tbsp. Olive Oil

Sauce:

- 1 tbsp. Korean Chili Flakes
- 1 tbsp. Honey

- 1 tbsp. Sugar
- ½ tbsp. Chili Paste
- ½ tsp minced Garlic
- 1 tbsp. Soy Sauce
- 1 tsp Rice Vinegar
- 1 tsp Sesame Oil

Preparation:

Cook the noodles following the package instructions, Drain and set them aside. Heat the oil in a pan over medium heat. Add onions and cook for 3 minutes. Add bacon and cook until crispy. Stir in kimchi and cook until wilted. Meanwhile, whisk together the sauce ingredients in a bowl.

Pour over the kimchi mixture. Stir in the noodles to coat well.

Indian Chicken Stir Fry

Love Indian food? Then I really have nothing else to say except that you will go absolutely crazy about this recipe. Creamy, gingery, garlicky, this stir fry is the ultimate definition of comfort food.

Serves: 4
Ready In: 20 minutes
Ingredients:

- 1 Bell Pepper, diced
- 4 tbsp. Olive Oil
- 1 tbsp. Cream
- ½ cup Yogurt
- 2 Chicken Breasts, chopped
- 1 Onion, diced
- 1 tbsp. Tomato Paste
- 1 Green Chili, chopped
- 1 tsp minced Garlic
- 2 tsp grated Ginger
- 1 tsp Cumin Powder

- ½ tsp Turmeric Powder
- 1 tsp Coriander
- ¼ tsp Red Chili Flakes
- ¼ tsp Salt

Preparation:

Heat half of the oil in wok over the medium heat. Add onions and pepper and cook for 2 minutes. Transfer to a plate. Heat the remaining oil and add the chicken. Cook until it is browned on all sides. Stir in all of the spices (the last 5 ingredients), and cook for 2 more minutes. Add the yogurt and cream. Stir in the remaining ingredients, including the onions and peppers. Cook for a few minutes.

Tomato Beef Stir Fry

Tomatoes, beef, and a hot wok are the stars of this amazing stir fry that you will not be able to resist. Great served with noodles, but even more irresistible over white rice. Give it a try and see for yourself.

Serves: 4
Ready In: 80 minutes
Ingredients:
Beef:

- 1 pound Flank Steak
- 1 tbsp. Cornstarch
- 1 tsp Oil
- ¼ tsp Salt

Stir-Fry:

- 3 tbsp. Oil
- 1 tsp minced Garlic
- 1 tbsp. Shaoxing Wine
- ½ tbsp. Cornstarch whisked with 1 tbsp. Water
- 2 Ginger Slices
- ¼ cup sliced Shallots
- 5 Tomatoes, chopped

Sauce:

- 2 tbsp. Ketchup
- 2 tbsp Soy Sauce

- ½ tsp Sesame Oil
- 1 ½ tsp Sugar

Preparation:
Combine the beef ingredients in a bowl. Cover and let marinate for 1 hour. Heat 1 tbsp oil in a hot wok and add the beef. Cook until browned on all sides. Transfer to a plate. Heat another tbsp of oil and add ginger. Add shallots and garlic and cook for another minute. Stir in the tomatoes and simmer for 2 minutes. Stir in the wine and give it a stir. Meanwhile whish together the sauce ingredients. Pour the mixture over the sauce. Stir in the beef. Cook until the sauce is thickened. Serve and enjoy!

Conclusion

See? I told you there were numerous ways in which you can prepare quick and easy and yet elegant and delectable stir fry. Now, all that you should do is heat your wok and start cooking.

Did you find these recipes tasty? Leave a review and let the others know. Your feedback will be greatly appreciated.

Thank you and happy stir frying!

Part 2

Introduction

It's hard to not get in on a cooking technique when it is known to produce gastronomic dishes in the quickest, simplest, easiest way possible. We're talking about stir-frying—a popular Asian cooking method that involves selecting fine ingredients to be tossed together in a wok to serve up flavorful and savory beef, pork, chicken, seafood and vegetable recipes.

Why Stir-fry?

Quite simply, stir-frying is a cooking technique used in most Asian kitchens that literally involves stirring choice ingredients over high heat. Originating in in China, the method is quite similar to the process of sautéing—where some cooking oil is used, followed by seasonings and is then followed by remaining ingredients. In most stir-fry recipes, a wok—which is a large, medium-deep dish typically made from thin stainless steel—is used to cook the dishes. Ingredients are constantly tossed and stirred around the wok over high heat, with expert chefs able to set the actual ingredients in the pot aflame, allowing food to be cooked even faster than the quick and easy method already does.

With that said—it's pretty obvious why stir-frying is the go-to technique used by anyone who wants to impress with their culinary skills but doesn't have the time to do so. It's quick, simple and tasty. All you need is a wok and a lot of creativity when it comes to mixing and matching ingredients that will define your signature stir-fry dish.

Benefits of Stir-fry

Apart from the obvious benefits of stir-frying—quick, easy and delicious recipes in a snap—few people really know about the nutritional benefits of this cooking technique. But there's more to stir-frying than meets the proverbial taste buds—

- Vegetables for instance are a top choice for stir-frying. Typically abhorred vegetables, especially by children, such as broccoli and cabbage can be recreated into something tasty. Here's a quick tip though. Most vegetables take longer to cook on a

wok, so it helps to blanch dense vegetables such as carrots and broccoli before you toss them in a wok.
- Choosing lean meats instead of fatty cuts can help lower the fat content of your easy meals.
- Stir-frying lends itself to lower oil retention because it uses chopped meats and veggies. Plus, Asian cooking typically used healthier oil options—peanut, olive, sesame to name a few.
- A big bonus for stir-frying is that it's easy to prep your ingredients the night before and all ready for cooking the next day.

Delicious Stir-Fry Recipes

Vegetables

Ginger And Asparagus Stir-Fry

Prep Time: **20 minutes**
Serves: 2-3

Ingredients:

2 pounds asparagus, cooked and cut into bite-sized pieces
2 teaspoons sesame seeds
2 tablespoons peanut oil
2 teaspoons ginger, grated
1/2 teaspoon salt
1 teaspoon sesame oil

Directions:

1. Toast sesame seeds using a non-stick pan until browned. Set aside.
2. Using the same pan, heat peanut oil and sauté ginger and asparagus.
3. Season with salt and continue to cook until fragrant.
4. Remove from heat and toss with sesame oil and seeds.

Classic Vegetable Stir-Fry

Prep Time: **20 minutes**
Serves: 2-3

Ingredients:

1 tablespoon olive oil
2 medium yellow squash, sliced
2 medium zucchini, sliced
1/2 package baby-cut carrots
1 medium red onion, cut in half and thickly sliced
2 packs vegetable broth flavoring

Directions:

1. Saute vegetables in a skillet with olive oil.
2. Add vegetable broth packs and cook until mixture is warmed through.

Peppered Brussels Sprouts

Prep Time: **40 minutes**
Serves: 2

Ingredients:

1 tablespoon vegetable oil
1 onion, chopped
1 potato, peeled and cubed
1 bay leaf
1 pound Brussels sprouts, trimmed and halved lengthwise
1 red pepper, seeded and diced
1/4 cup chicken broth
Black pepper, to taste
2 tablespoons chopped green onions

Directions:

1. Saute onions and potatoes with the bay leaf in vegetable oil.
2. Cook until tender and add remaining ingredients.
3. Cover and cook fro about 10 minutes.
4. Once ready, remove bay leaf and remove form heat.
5. Toss with pepper and green onions.

Garlic And Bitter Melon Stir-Fry

Prep Time: **15 minutes**
Serves: 1

Ingredients:

2 tablespoons olive oil
1 small onion, diced
2 cloves garlic, crushed
1 tomato, chopped
salt and pepper to taste
1 bitter melon, seeded and sliced
1 large tomato, seeded and diced

Directions:

1. Saute garlic and onions in oil until tender.
2. Add tomatoes and bitter melon.
3. Cook until tender.

Asian Bok Choy Toss

Prep Time: **15 minutes**
Serves: 2

Ingredients:

1 large head bok choy, stemmed and sliced into bite-sized pieces; leaves torn into bit- sized pieces
1 tablespoon grapeseed oil
1 tablespoon butter
1 onion, sliced
1/3 cup cashews
3 cloves garlic, minced
1/2 teaspoon Chinese five-spice powder, or more to taste
1 pinch white sugar

Directions:

1. Saute all ingredients together in a large wok.
2. Toss together to make sure spices and sugar are evenly distributed.

Soy Cabbage Stir-Fry

Prep Time: **10 minutes**
Serves: 3-4

Ingredients:

1 tablespoon vegetable oil
2 tablespoons minced onion
2 cloves garlic, minced
6 cups chopped cabbage
1 tablespoon soy sauce
1/2 teaspoon white sugar
1/8 teaspoon ground black pepper

Directions:

1. Suate onions and garlic in a wok in vegetable oil.
2. Add cabbage and cook for about 5 minutes.
3. Lower heat and add soy sauce.
4. Season with black pepper.

Tomato And Egg Stir-Fry

Prep Time: **10 minutes**
Serves: 3-4

Ingredients:

2 tablespoons vegetable oil
6 eggs, beaten
1 green onion, chopped
2 large tomatoes cut into thin wedges
salt to taste

Directions:

1. Saute onions and tomatoes in oil.
2. Add eggs and add tomatoes.
3. Season with salt and toss together.

Beef

Sirloin Stir-Fry

Prep Time: **40 minutes**
Serves: 4

Ingredients:

2 pounds boneless beef sirloin, sliced into strips
3 tablespoons cornstarch
1 can beef broth
1/2 cup soy sauce
2 tablespoons sugar
2 tablespoons vegetable oil
4 cups sliced mushrooms
1 head Chinese cabbage, thinly sliced
2 medium red peppers, cut into strips
3 stalks celery, sliced
2 medium green onions, cut into bite-sized pieces

Hot cooked regular white rice

Directions:

1. In a bowl, whisk together broth, soy sauce, cornstarch and sugar.
2. Heat oil in a wok and sauté beef until brown.
3. Add mushrooms, peppers, celery, green onions and cabbage.
4. Add cornstarch mixture and continue to cook until mixture is thick.
5. Serve mixture over hot rice.

Beef And Peas Stir-Fry

Prep Time: **90 minutes**
Serves: 4

Ingredients:

2 cups brown rice, cooked
4 cups water
2 tablespoons cornstarch
2 teaspoons white sugar
6 tablespoons soy sauce
1/4 cup white wine
1 tablespoon minced fresh ginger
1 pound boneless beef round steak, cut into thin strips
1 tablespoon vegetable oil
3 cups broccoli florets
2 carrots, thinly sliced
1 (6 ounce) package frozen pea pods, thawed
2 tablespoons chopped onion
1 (8 ounce) can sliced water chestnuts, undrained
1 cup Chinese cabbage
2 large heads bok choy, chopped
1 tablespoon vegetable oil

Directions:

1. Whisk sugar, soy sauce, wine and cornstarch in a bowl with ginger. Add beef and marinate for an hour.
2. Heat oil in a wok and sauté remaining ingredients together. Allow mixture to simmer until vegetables are tender.
3. Pour beef mixture in and lower heat. Keep stirring until mixture is thick.
4. Serve over rice.

Garlic And Beef Stir-Fry

Prep Time: **30 minutes**
Serves: 4

Ingredients:

1 tablespoon butter
1/2 pound beef strips
2 cloves garlic, minced
1/4 sweet onion, chopped
2 teaspoons teriyaki sauce

Directions:

1. Melt butter in a wok over high heat.
2. Saute onions and garlic until fragrant.
3. Add beef strips and toss with butter to coat well.
4. Add teriyaki sauce and toss ingredients together well.

Beef In Oyster Sauce Stir-Fry

Prep Time: **30 minutes**
Serves: 4

Ingredients:

2 tablespoons butter
1 pound beef strips
2 cloves garlic, minced
2 cups button mushrooms, sliced thin
2 tablespoons oyster sauce

Directions:

1. Saute garlic in butter in a wok.
2. Add beef strips and toss pieces to coat well with garlic butter mixture.
3. Add mushrooms and oyster sauce.
4. Season with salt and pepper and serve.

Beef And Baby Corn Stir-Fry

Prep Time: **30 minutes**
Serves: 2

Ingredients:

2 tablespoon butter
1 can baby corn, drained
1/2 pound beef strips
2 cloves garlic, minced
1 red onion, diced
2 teaspoons oyster sauce

Directions:

1. Saute garlic with corn and onions in butter.
2. Once fragrant, add beef strips.
3. Add oyster sauce and toss to mix through.

Beef And Broccoli Stir-Fry

Prep Time: **30 minutes**
Serves: **4**

Ingredients:

2 tablespoons vegetable oil
1 pound beef sirloin, cut into strips
1 1/2 cups fresh broccoli florets
1 red bell pepper, cut into thin strips
2 carrots, cut into thin strips
1 green onion, chopped
1 teaspoon minced garlic
2 tablespoons soy sauce
2 tablespoons sesame seeds, toasted

Directions:

1. Suate beef in oil in a wok.
2. Add vegetables and garlic.
3. Toss ingredients together with soy sauce and sesame seeds.
4. Allow to cook until vegetables are tender.

Peppered Sesame Beef Stir-Fry

Prep Time: **20 minutes**
Serves: **4**

Ingredients:

1 tablespoon butter
6 tablespoons sesame oil
2 tablespoons sesame seeds
1/2 pound beef strips
2 cloves garlic, minced
1 tablespoon soy sauce
1 tablespoon fresh ground pepper

Directions:

1. Melt butter in a wok and add onions and garlic.
2. Add beef strips and season with pepper.
3. Toss well and drizzle with sesame oil and seeds.

Ponzu Sauce Beef Toss

Prep Time: **30 minutes**
Serves: 4

Ingredients:

2 tablespoons ponzu sauce
2 tablespoons sesame seeds
1/2 pound beef strips
2 cloves garlic, minced
1 tablespoon soy sauce

Directions:

1. Combine all ingredients together in a wok.
2. Toss around and stir ingredients constantly to distribute the flavors evenly.

Chili Beef Stir-Fry

Prep Time: **30 minutes**
Serves: 4

Ingredients:

2 tablespoons sesame oil
2 tablespoons Sriracha hot sauce
1/2 pound beef strips
2 cloves garlic, minced
1 teaspoon chili flakes

Directions:

1. Combine all ingredients together in a wok.
2. Toss around and stir ingredients constantly to distribute the flavors evenly.

Beef And Cilantro Stir-Fry

Prep Time: **30 minutes**
Serves: 4

Ingredients:

2 tablespoons sesame oil
1 tablespoon dried cilantro
Handful of fresh cilantro, chopped
1/2 pound beef strips
2 cloves garlic, minced
1 tablespoon soy sauce

Directions:

1. Combine all ingredients together in a wok.
2. Toss around and stir ingredients constantly to distribute the flavors evenly.

Pork

Peppered Pork Stir-Fry

Prep Time: **50 minutes**
Serves: 4

Ingredients:

1/4 cup rice wine vinegar
2 tablespoons minced garlic
1 tablespoon brown sugar
5 tablespoons olive oil
salt and pepper to taste
4 boneless pork loin chops, cut into bite sized pieces
5 tablespoons vegetable oil
3 tablespoons fresh ginger root, finely chopped
1 tablespoon hot chile paste
5 tablespoons teriyaki sauce
1 green bell pepper, cut into strips
1 red bell pepper, cut into strips
1 yellow bell pepper, cut into strips

salt and pepper to taste
1/4 cup blanched slivered almonds
2 tablespoons chopped fresh mint

Directions:

1. Whisk together vinegar, brown sugar, garlic, oil, seasoned with salt and pepper. Add pork and allow to marinate for at least half an hour.
2. Once ready to cook, toast almonds in a wok until browned.
3. Add all remaining ingredients and toss together well.

Wansoy Pork Stir-Fry

Prep Time: **50 minutes**
Serves: 2-4

Ingredients:

1/4 cup olive oil
1/2 cup finely chopped fresh cilantro leaves
1 tablespoon finely chopped ginger
4 cloves garlic, finely chopped
1 pound pork tenderloin, thinly sliced
2 tablespoons olive oil, divided
2 onions, thinly sliced
1 red bell pepper, thinly sliced
1 tablespoon lime juice

Directions:

1. Combine ginger, cilantro, garlic and olive oil in a bowl. Add pork and allow to marinate for half an hour, at least.
2. Once ready, take pork pieces and sauté in a wok with olive oil until browned.
3. Take 2 tablespoons of the marinade and add into the wok.
4. Add remaining ingredients and stir until cooked through.

Vietnamese Pork Stir-Fry

Prep Time: **50 minutes**
Serves: 4

Ingredients:

1/4 cup olive oil
4 cloves garlic, minced
1 fresh ginger root, minced
1/4 cup fish sauce
1/4 cup reduced-sodium soy sauce
1 dash sesame oil
2 pounds pork tenderloin, thinly sliced
1 tablespoon vegetable oil
2 cloves garlic, minced
3 green onions, cut into 2 inch pieces
1 large onion, thinly sliced
2 cups frozen whole green beans, partially thawed
1/2 cup reduced-sodium beef broth
2 tablespoons lime juice
1 tablespoon chopped fresh Thai basil
1 tablespoon chopped fresh mint
1 pinch red pepper flakes, or to taste
1/2 teaspoon ground black pepper

Directions:

1. Whisk garlic, ginger, olive oil, fish sauce, soy sauce and sesame oil together. Add pork pieces and allow to marinate for at least half an hour.
2. Once ready to cook, sauté pork in a wok until browned. Add remaining ingredients and continue stirring until mixture is cooked through.

Pineapple And Pork Stir-Fry

Prep Time: **50 minutes**
Serves: 4

Ingredients:

1 can pineapple chunks - drained with juice reserved
2 teaspoons rice wine vinegar
2 tablespoons soy sauce
1 teaspoon olive oil
1/2 teaspoon ground ginger
1/2 teaspoon brown sugar
1/2 teaspoon white sugar
1 (1 1/2-pound) pork strips
1 1/2 cups water
1/2 cup white rice, cooked
2 tablespoons olive oil

Directions:

1. Combine pineapple juice, soy sauce, olive oil, rice wine, ginger, sugars with a whisk.
2. Add pork pieces and allow to marinate for half an hour.
3. Once ready to cook, sauté pork in a wok until browned. Add remaining ingredients, except rice, and continue stirring until mixture is cooked through.

4. Serve over cooked rice

Perfect Pork Stir-Fry

Prep Time: 5 hours 15 minutes
Serves: 8

Ingredients:

2 teaspoons chopped fresh ginger root
1 clove garlic, minced
1 teaspoon fish sauce
1 teaspoon soy sauce
2 teaspoons miso paste
1 teaspoon sesame oil
1 tablespoon vegetable oil
1/2 pound pork strips
1 cup snow peas
1 cup broccoli, chopped
1 cup bok choy, chopped
1 cup chopped green bell pepper
1 cup bean sprouts
1 cup chopped zucchini

Directions:

1. Combine together the ginger, garlic, soy sauce, fish sauce, miso paste, and sesame oil in a bowl. Add pork strips and allow to marinate for half an hour.

2. Once ready to cook, sauté pork in a wok until browned. Add remaining ingredients and continue stirring until mixture is cooked through.

Peppered Pork And Peas Stir-Fry

Prep Time: **40 minutes**
Serves: 4

Ingredients:

1 pound pork strips
2 tablespoons cornstarch
2 tablespoons soy sauce
1 1/2 teaspoons white sugar
3 tablespoons olive oil
1 sweet onion, chopped
2 cloves garlic, crushed
1 tablespoon oyster sauce
salt and pepper to taste
1 pound snow peas
3/4 cup green peas
1 carrot, sliced
2 stalks celery, sliced
1 red bell pepper, seeded and cut into chunks
1/4 cup oil for deep frying

Directions:

1. Toss pork slices with cornstarch.
2. Combine sugar and soy sauce and pour over beef slices. Marinate for half an hour.

3. Once ready to cook, sauté pork in a wok until browned. Add remaining ingredients and continue stirring until mixture is cooked through.

Pork And Ginger Wok Toss

Prep Time: **50 minutes**
Serves: 4

Ingredients:

2 tablespoons vegetable oil
1/2 inch piece fresh ginger root, thinly sliced
1/4 pound thinly sliced lean pork
1 teaspoon soy sauce
1/2 teaspoon dark soy sauce
1/2 teaspoon salt
1/3 teaspoon sugar
1 teaspoon sesame oil
1 green onion, chopped
1 tablespoon Chinese rice wine

Directions:

1. Saute ginger in oil in a wok.
2. Add all remaining ingredients together and toss together well.
3. Allow mixture to simmer until tender.

Cauliflower And Ham Stir-Fry

Prep Time: **30 minutes**
Serves: 4

Ingredients:

1 1/2 cups water
2 cups chicken broth
1/4 cup cornstarch
3 tablespoons soy sauce
3 tablespoons brown sugar
1/8 teaspoon ground ginger
1 tablespoon vegetable oil
2 cloves garlic, minced
1 (16 ounce) package mixed broccoli and cauliflower florets
1 carrot, sliced
1/4 pound cooked ham, cut into strips
1/2 cup sliced almonds

Directions:

1. Using a wok, sauté vegetables together in oil.
2. Pour broth and add ham.
3. Mix thoroughly and toss with almonds.

Spicy Pork Strips Stir-Fry

Prep Time: **35 minutes**
Serves: 4

Ingredients:

2 tablespoons soy sauce
1 tablespoon cornstarch
1 tablespoon water
1 pound pork tenderloin, cubed
1 lime, juiced
1 tablespoon soy sauce
2 tablespoons rice vinegar
1 teaspoon cornstarch
3 teaspoons dark sesame oil
1 tablespoon peanut oil
3 teaspoons minced fresh ginger root
2 green chile peppers, chopped
1/2 cup julienned carrots
1/2 cup sugar snap peas, julienned
2 teaspoons chili oil
1/4 cup chopped green onions
1/4 cup finely chopped peanuts

Directions:

1. Saute pork pieces in oil until browned.

2. One by one, add remaining ingredients, except peanuts, and cook thoroughly.
3. Once ready, remove form heat and toss with peanuts.

Peaches And Pork Stir-Fry

Prep Time: **40 minutes**
Serves: 2-4

Ingredients:

1/4 cup lemon juice
1/4 cup soy sauce
1/2 teaspoon ground ginger
1/2 teaspoon garlic powder
1 pound cubed pork meat
2 teaspoons peanut oil, or sesame oil
1 large onion, diced
1 large carrot, sliced
1 cup broccoli florets
1 (15 ounce) can sliced peaches, with juice

Directions:

1. Whisk together lemon juice, ginger, soy sauce and garlic powder. Add pork and allow to marinade.
2. Marinate for half an hour.
3. Once ready to cook, sauté pork in a wok until browned. Add remaining ingredients and continue stirring until mixture is cooked through.

Chicken

Ginger Chicken Stir-Fry

Prep Time: **45 minutes**
Serves: 4

Ingredients:

2 teaspoons cornstarch
1 1/2 cups chicken broth
2 tablespoons low-sodium soy sauce
2 teaspoons lemon juice
2 teaspoons fresh grated ginger
2 tablespoons vegetable oil
1 pound skinless, boneless chicken breast, cut into strips
4 cups broccoli florets
2 medium carrots, sliced
1 small onion, chopped

1/4 cup chopped fresh cilantro leaves
3 cups hot cooked regular brown rice or regular long-grain white rice

Directions:

1. Whisk broth with cornstarch, lemon juice, soy sauce and ginger together. Add chicken and allow to marinate for half an hour.
2. Once ready, sauté chicken with remaining ingredients.

Pecan Chicken Stir-Fry

Prep Time: **35 minutes**
Serves: 2-4

Ingredients:

1 tablespoon extra virgin olive oil
4 skinless, boneless chicken breast halves - cut into strips
1 cup julienned carrots
1 small onion, chopped
1 cup fresh sliced mushrooms
1 zucchini squash, peeled and cut into 1 inch rounds
2 yellow summer squash, peeled and sliced into 1 inch pieces
1/2 cup pecan halves
1 teaspoon coarse ground black pepper

Directions:

1. Saute chicken in hot oil and cook until brown.
2. Add remaining ingredients and continue to stir until cooked through.
3. Season with salt and pepper.

Garlic Chicken Asian Toss

Prep Time: **40 minutes**
Serves: **2-4**

Ingredients:

2 tablespoons peanut oil
6 cloves garlic, minced
1 teaspoon grated fresh ginger
1 bunch green onions, chopped
1 teaspoon salt
1 pound boneless skinless chicken breasts, cut into strips
2 onions, thinly sliced
1 cup sliced cabbage
1 red bell pepper, thinly sliced
2 cups sugar snap peas
1 cup chicken broth
2 tablespoons soy sauce
2 tablespoons white sugar
2 tablespoons cornstarch

Directions:

1. Saute garlic, green onions, ginger and salt over high heat.
2. Add chicken until bronwed.

3. Add remaining ingredients and continue stirring until mixture is thick.

Orange Chicken Chow Mein

Prep Time: **40 minutes**
Serves: **2-4**

Ingredients:

1 cup orange juice
1 tablespoon grated orange zest
1/4 cup soy sauce
1 teaspoon salt
3 cloves garlic, chopped
1 tablespoon brown sugar
3 tablespoons vegetable oil
4 skinless, boneless chicken breast halves - cut into 1 inch cubes
2 tablespoons all-purpose flour
1 cup bean sprouts (optional)
1 (6 ounce) package crispy chow mein noodles

Directions:

1. Whisk orange zest with juice, soy sauce, garlic and brown sugar. Season with salt and mix well.
2. Heat oil in a wok, add chicken and cook until brown.

3. Add orange sauce into the wok and allow to simmer.
4. Stir in flour slowly until mixture thicken.
5. Add sprouts and noodles.
6. Toss well to coat evenly and serve.

Seafood

Basil Shrimp Stir-Fry

Prep Time: **40 minutes**
Serves: 2-4

Ingredients:

1 tablespoon soy sauce
2 tablespoons water
1 tablespoon white sugar
2 pounds shrimp
1 tablespoon vegetable oil
5 green onions, sliced
3 cloves garlic, chopped
3 tablespoons vegetable oil
2 (6 ounce) bags fresh baby spinach leaves
1 cup thinly sliced fresh basil

Directions:

1. Mix soy sauce, water, and sugar in a bowl. Place chicken in a bowl and allow to marinate for half an hour.
2. Once ready, sauté with all remaining ingredients until cooked through.

Salt And Pepper Salmon Toss

Prep Time: **40 minutes**
Serves: 4

Ingredients:

1 tablespoon flaked sea salt
2 teaspoons finely cracked black pepper
1 teaspoon crushed red pepper flakes, or to taste
1 teaspoon Chinese five-spice powder
1 teaspoon ground paprika
1 tablespoon vegetable oil
4 skinless salmon fillets
1 pound broccoli florets, cut in half
3 small carrots, peeled and cut into matchstick-sized pieces

Directions:

1. Combine red pepper flakes, black pepper, five-spice, sea salt and paprika.
2. In a wok, cook salmon and crumble.
3. Add remaining ingredients and stir until cooked through.

Caribbean Shrimp Stir-Fry

Prep Time: **15 minutes**
Serves: 4

Ingredients:

1 tablespoon vegetable oil
1 green bell pepper, seeded and cubed
1 red bell pepper, seeded and cubed
1/4 cup sliced sweet onions
3/4 pound shrimp, peeled and chopped
2 1/2 teaspoons Caribbean jerk seasoning
1/2 cup plum sauce
1 tablespoon soy sauce
1/4 cup chopped roasted peanuts

Directions:

1. Suate shrimp in a wok.
2. Add pepper and onions and jerk seasoning.
3. Pour sauce into the wok and add remaining ingredients.
4. Cook until vegetables are tender.

Curry Shrimp Stir-Fry

Prep Time: **35 minutes**
Serves: 2-4

Ingredients:

1/4 cup butter
1 teaspoon cumin seeds
1 pound shrimp, peeled
2 tablespoons vegetable oil
1 large onion, finely chopped
2 large carrots, thinly sliced
4 cloves garlic, diced
1 tablespoon grated ginger
2 teaspoons crushed red pepper flakes
1 teaspoon honey
1 teaspoon ground cumin
1/2 teaspoon curry powder, or more to taste
salt and ground black pepper to taste

Directions:

1. Saute cumin seeds with butter in a wok.
2. Add shrimp and cook thoroughly.
3. Add all remaining ingredients and keep stirring until flavorings are mixed thoroughly.

Stir Fry Recipes

Mushroom & Bell Peppers Stir Fry

Servings: **4**
Preparation Time: **20 minutes**
Cooking Time: **11 minutes**
Ingredients:
- 2 tablespoons olive oil
- 3 scallions, chopped
- 2 garlic cloves, minced
- 1 medium tomato, chopped finely
- 2 medium green bell peppers, seeded and sliced
- 2 medium red bell peppers, seeded and sliced
- ¾ cup fresh button mushrooms, sliced
- ¾ cup fresh crimini mushrooms, sliced
- 2 tablespoons Worcestershire sauce
- ½ tablespoon balsamic vinegar
- ½ teaspoon honey
- Salt and freshly ground black pepper, to taste
- 2 tablespoons fresh basil leaves, chopped

Directions:

1. In a large skillet, heat oil on medium heat.
2. Add scallions and garlic and stir fry for about 2-3 minutes.

3. Add tomato and cook for 2 minutes, breaking the tomatoes with the back of spoon.
4. Add bell pepper and mushrooms and stir fry for about 2-3 minutes.
5. Add remaining ingredients and stir fry for about 2-3 minutes more.

Nutritional Information (Per Serving):
Calories: 126
Fat: 7.5g
Sat Fat: 1.1g
Sodium: 93mg
Carbohydrates: **13.0g**
Fiber: **3.4g**
Sugar: **8.8g**
Protein: **2.5g**

Broccoli & Bell Pepper Stir Fry

Servings: 4
Preparation Time: 20 minutes
Cooking Time: **10 minutes**
Ingredients:

- 2 tablespoons olive oil
- 2 garlic cloves, minced
- 1 large onion, chopped
- 2 cups broccoli small florets
- 1 large red bell pepper, seeded and cubed
- 1 large yellow bell pepper, seeded and cubed
- 1 large green bell pepper, seeded and cubed
- ¼ cup vegetable broth
- Sea salt and freshly ground black pepper, to taste

Directions:

1. In a large skillet, heat oil on medium heat.
2. Add garlic and sauté for about 1 minute.
3. Add vegetables and stir fry for about 4-5 minutes.
4. Add broth and stir fry for about 3-4 minutes more.
5. Serve hot.

Nutritional Information (Per Serving):

Calories: **133**
Fat: **7.7g**
Sat Fat: **1.1g**

Sodium: **69**mg
Carbohydrates: **14.5g**
Fiber: **4.6g**
Sugar: **7.6g**
Protein: **3.3g**

Cauliflower Stir Fry

Servings: **4**
Preparation Time: **20 minutes**
Cooking Time: **7 minutes**

Ingredients:
- 2 teaspoons vegetable oil
- 2 garlic cloves, minced
- 1 head cauliflower, cut into florets
- 2 scallions, chopped
- 2 tablespoons fresh lime juice
- 2 tablespoons soy sauce
- 1 tablespoon Sriracha

Directions:
1. In a large skillet, heat oil on medium-high heat.
2. Add garlic and sauté for about 1 minute.
3. Add cauliflower and stir fry for about 3-4 minutes.
4. Reduce the heat to low.
5. Add scallions, lime juice and soy sauce and stir fry for about 1 minute.
6. Stir in hot sauce and stir fry for 1 minute more.
7. Serve hot.

Nutritional Information (Per Serving):
Calories: **55**
Fat: **2.4g**
Sat Fat: **0g**
Sodium: **499mg**
Carbohydrates: **7.8g**

Fiber: **2.0g**
Sugar: **2.3g**
Protein: **2.1g**

Kale Stir Fry

Servings: **2**
Preparation Time: **10 minutes**
Cooking Time: **7 minutes**

Ingredients:
- 1 tablespoon olive oil
- 1 garlic clove, minced
- 1 tablespoon fresh ginger, minced
- 1/8 teaspoon red pepper flakes, crushed
- ½ pound fresh kale, trimmed and chopped roughly
- 1/3 cup water
- 2 teaspoons soy sauce
- 3 teaspoons sesame seeds, toasted

Directions:
1. In a large skillet, heat oil on medium-high heat.
2. Add garlic, ginger and red pepper flakes and sauté for about 1 minute.
3. Add kale and stir fry for about 1-2 minutes.
4. Add water and soy sauce and stir fry for about 3-4 minutes.
5. Garnish with sesame seeds and serve warm.

Nutritional Information (Per Serving):
Calories: **156**
Fat: **9.4g**
Sat Fat: **1.4g**
Sodium: **351mg**
Carbohydrates: **15.8 g**

Fiber: **2.7g**
Sugar: **0g**
Protein: **4.9g**

Broccoli & Zucchini Stir Fry

Servings: **2**
Preparation Time: **10 minutes**
Cooking Time: **8 minutes**
Ingredients:

- 1 tablespoons olive oil
- 1 garlic clove, minced
- 1 serrano pepper, seeded and chopped
- 1 cup small broccoli florets
- 2 medium zucchinis, spiralized with blade C
- ¼ cup soy sauce
- Salt and freshly ground black pepper, to taste
- 1 tablespoon black sesame seeds, toasted

Directions:

1. In a large nonstick skillet, heat oil on medium heat.
2. Add garlic and serrano pepper and sauté for about 1 minute.
3. Add broccoli and stir fry for about 2 minutes.
4. Add zucchini and soy sauce and stir fry for about 4-5 minutes.
5. Garnish with sesame seeds and serve.

Nutritional Information (Per Serving):
Calories: **153**
Fat: **9.8**g
Sat Fat: **1.4**g
Sodium: **1833**mg
Carbohydrates: **13.8**g

Fiber: **4.3g**
Sugar: **4.8g**
Protein: **6.6g**

Spicy Potato Stir Fry

Servings: 6
Preparation Time: **10 minutes**
Cooking Time: **8 minutes**

Ingredients:
- 3 tablespoons canola oil
- 1 tablespoon yellow mustard seeds
- 1 medium onion, chopped
- 3 garlic cloves, minced
- 1 jalapeño pepper, seeded and chopped
- 2 teaspoons ground cumin
- 2 teaspoons ground coriander
- ¼ teaspoon red pepper flakes, crushed
- 6 medium red potatoes, peeled, cubed, soaked in water for 10 minutes and drained
- Salt, to taste
- 2 tablespoons fresh lemon juice
- ½ cup fresh cilantro leaves, chopped
- ½ cup fresh mint leaves, chopped

Directions:
1. In a large skillet, heat oil on medium heat.
2. Add mustard seeds and stir fry for about 1 minute.
3. Add onion and stir fry for about 4-5 minutes.
4. Add garlic, jalapeño and spices and stir fry for about 1 minute.
5. Add potatoes and stir fry for about 3-4 minutes.

6. Reduce the heat to low. Cover and cook, stirring occasionally for about 12-15 minutes or till done completely.
7. Stir in salt, lemon juice and herbs and cook for 1 minute more.
8. Remove from heat but keep aside covered for about 5-10 minutes before serving.

Nutritional Information (Per Serving):
Calories: **238**
Fat: **8.2g**
Sat Fat: **0.7g**
Sodium: **46mg**
Carbohydrates: **38.0g**
Fiber: **5.1g**
Sugar: **3.3g**
Protein: **5.3g**

Sesame Beef Stir Fry

Servings: **4**
Preparation Time: **10** minutes
Cooking Time: **7 minutes**
Ingredients:
- 2 scallions, chopped
- 2 garlic cloves, ,minced
- ¼ cup white Sugar
- ¼ cup soy sauce
- 3 tablespoons olive oil
- 1 pound round steak, cut into thin strips
- 2 tablespoons sesame seeds

Directions:
1. In a large bowl, mix together all ingredients except steak.
2. Add steak and coat with marinade generously.
3. Cover and refrigerate for about 6-8 hours.
4. Heat a large nonstick skillet on medium heat.
5. Add beef with marinade and stir fry for about 5-7 minutes or till done completely.
6. Stir in sesame seeds and serve.

Nutritional Information (Per Serving):
Calories: **421**
Fat: **23.7g**
Sat Fat: **5.9g**
Sodium: **969**mg
Carbohydrates: **15.8g**

Fiber: **0.9g**
Sugar: **13.0g**
Protein: **36.2g**

Ginger & Chiles Beef Stir Fry

Servings: **6**
Preparation Time: **10 minutes**
Cooking Time: **6 minutes**

Ingredients:

For Ginger Marinade:
- 1 tablespoon fresh ginger, grated finely
- 5 tablespoons soy sauce
- 2 tablespoons rice vinegar
- 1 tablespoons honey
- 1 teaspoon ground cumin
- 1 teaspoon red pepper flakes, crushed
- 1 ½ pounds top sirloin steak, cut into ½-inch thick strips

For Stir Fry:
- 1 tablespoon cornstarch
- 2 tablespoons water
- 1 tablespoon sesame oil
- 2 tablespoons peanut oil
- 2 serrano chiles, seeded and sliced
- 2 garlic cloves, minced
- 1 tablespoon fresh ginger, julienned
- ½ cup fresh cilantro, chopped

Direction
1. For beef in a large bowl, mix together all ingredients except steak.
2. Add steak and coat with marinade generously.
3. Cover and refrigerate for about 4-6 hours.

4. In a bowl, mix together cornstarch and water. Keep aside.
5. In a large skillet, heat both oils on medium-high heat.
6. Add beef and stir fry for about 2-3 minutes. Transfer beef into a bowl.
7. In the same skillet, add serrano and garlic and stir fry for about 30 seconds.
8. Add ginger and stir fry for about 30 seconds.
9. Stir in beef with ginger mixture and stir fry for 1 minute.
10. Stir in cornstarch mixture. Cook, stirring continuously for about 2 minutes more.
11. **Stir in cilantro and serve.**

Nutritional Information (Per Serving):
Calories: **307**
Fat: **14.1g**
Sat Fat: **3.8g**
Sodium: **860mg**
Carbohydrates: **7.4g**
Fiber: **0.6g**
Sugar: **3.2g**
Protein: **35.6g**

Beef & Orange Stir Fry

Servings: **4**
Preparation Time: **10 minutes**
Cooking Time: **8 minutes**

Ingredients:

For Beef Marinade:
- **2 garlic cloves, minced**
- **¼ cup rice vinegar**
- **¼ cup fresh orange juice**
- **2 tablespoon soy sauce**
- **1 tablespoon brown sugar**
- **1 tablespoon hot sauce**
- **1 pound beef tenderloin, cut into ½-inch thick strips**

For Stir Fry:
- **1 teaspoon cornstarch**
- **¼ cup water**
- **1 tablespoon olive oil**
- **2 tablespoon fresh orange zest, grated finely**
- **2 large scallions, chopped**
- **Salt and freshly ground black pepper, to taste**

Direction
1. For beef in a large bowl, mix together all ingredients except steak.
2. Add steak and coat with marinade generously.
3. Cover and refrigerate for about 2-3 hours.

4. Arrange a colander over a bowl. Remove beef from refrigerator and transfer into colander. Keep aside for 5 minutes. Reserve the marinade.
5. In a bowl, mix together cornstarch and water. Keep aside.
6. In a large skillet, heat oil on medium-high heat.
7. Add beef and stir fry for about 2 minutes.
8. Stir in orange zest and scallion and stir fry for about 1 minute.
9. Add reserved marinade and cook for about 2-3 minutes.
10. **Stir in salt and black pepper and remove from heat.**

Nutritional Information (Per Serving):
Calories: **266**
Fat: **10.4g**
Sat Fat: **4.0g**
Sodium: **614**mg
Carbohydrates: **5.0g**
Fiber: **0g**
Sugar: **3.7g**
Protein: **33.6g**

Beef & Green Beans Stir Fry

Servings: 4
Preparation Time: 15 minutes
Cooking Time: **15 minutes**
Ingredients:
- ½ tablespoon olive oil
- 1 pound skirt steak, cut into thin strips
- 1 tablespoon fresh ginger, grated
- 4 garlic cloves, minced
- 1 pound fresh green beans, trimmed and cut into 2-inch pieces
- 2 tablespoons soy sauce
- ¼ cup fresh cilantro leaves, chopped
- Salt and freshly ground black pepper, to taste

Directions:
1. In a large skillet, heat oil on medium-high heat.
2. Add steak and stir fry for about 4-5 minutes. Transfer the steak into a plate.
3. In the same skillet, add garlic and ginger and sauté for 1 minute.
4. Add beans and stir fry for about 6-7 minutes.
5. Add steak, soy sauce and cilantro and cook for 1-2 minutes.
6. Season with salt and black pepper and serve hot.

Nutritional Information (Per Serving):
Calories: **296**
Fat: **13.4g**

Sat Fat: **4.7g**
Sodium: **545**mg
Carbohydrates: **10.7 g**
Fiber: **4.2g**
Sugar: **1.8g**
Protein: **33.1g**

Beef & Mushroom Stir Fry

Servings: **3**
Preparation Time: **15 minutes**
Cooking Time: **12 minutes**

Ingredients:

For Beef Marinade:
- 1 teaspoon vegetable oil
- ½ teaspoon soy sauce
- ½ teaspoon white wine
- ½ teaspoon cornstarch
- ¼ teaspoon sugar
- Salt and freshly ground black pepper, to taste
- ½ pound flank steak, cut into 1/8-inch thick slices

For Stir Fry:
- 3 tablespoons vegetable oil, divided
- 1 teaspoon fresh ginger, minced
- 2 garlic cloves, minced
- ½ pound mixed fresh mushrooms, sliced
- 1 tablespoon unsalted butter
- 2 teaspoons soy sauce

Direction
1. For beef in a large bowl, mix together all ingredients except steak.
2. Add steak and coat with marinade generously.
3. Cover and refrigerate for about 30-40 minutes.
4. In a large skillet, heat 2 tablespoons of oil on medium-high heat.
5. Add ginger and garlic and sauté for about 1 minute.

6. Add beef and stir fry for about 2-3 minutes. Transfer beef into a bowl.
7. In the same skillet, heat remaining oil on medium-high heat.
8. Add mushrooms and stir fry for about 5 minutes or till all liquid is evaporated.
9. Add butter and soy sauce and stir fry for about 1 minute.
10. Add beef and stir fry for 1-2 minutes more.

Nutritional Information (Per Serving):
Calories: **341**
Fat: **25.5g**
Sat Fat: **8.0g**
Sodium: **323**mg
Carbohydrates: **4.7g**
Fiber: **0.9g**
Sugar: **1.8g**
Protein: **23.9g**

Ground Beef, Bell Pepper& Cabbage Stir Fry

Servings:**4**
Preparation Time: **15 minutes**
Cooking Time: **20 minutes**
Ingredients:
- 1 teaspoon cornstarch
- ½ cup water
- 2 tablespoons olive oil
- 4 garlic cloves, minced
- ½ pound ground beef
- 1 red bell pepper, seeded and cut into thin strips
- ½ of small head cabbage, shredded
- 2 tablespoons soy sauce
- Freshly ground black pepper, to taste

Directions:
1. In a bowl, mix together cornstarch and water. Keep aside.
2. In a large skillet, heat oil on medium-high heat.
3. Add garlic and sauté for about 1 minute.
4. Add beef and stir fry for about 4-5 minutes or till browned.
5. Add bell pepper and cabbage and stir fry for about 8-10 minutes.
6. Add soy sauce and cornstarch mixture and cook for about 2-4 minutes.
7. Season with black pepper and remove from heat.

Nutritional Information (Per Serving):

Calories: **208**
Fat: **10.7**g
Sat Fat: **2.4g**
Sodium: **507**mg
Carbohydrates: **9.2g**
Fiber: **3.0g**
Sugar: **4.3g**
Protein: **19.3g**

Chicken, Veggies & Fruit Stir Fry

Servings: **4**
Preparation Time: **10 minutes**
Cooking Time: **13 minutes**

Ingredients:

For Sauce:
- 2/3 cup chicken broth
- 1 tablespoon water
- 2 tablespoons light soy sauce
- ½ teaspoon sugar
- 2 teaspoons cornstarch

For Stir Fry:
- 2 tablespoons canola oil, divide
- 3 (4-ounce) skinless, boneless chicken breasts, cut into bite sized pieces
- 1 medium carrot, peeled and julienned
- 4-ounce snow peas, trimmed
- 1 medium red apple, cored and cubed
- 8 dried figs, chopped
- 1 large scallion, chopped
- 2 cups bok choy, cut into 1-inch pieces

Directions:
1. For sauce in a bowl, mix together all ingredients. Keep aside.
2. In a large heat 1 tablespoon oil on medium-high heat.
3. Add chicken and stir fry for about 4-5 minutes or till browned from all seeds.

4. Transfer the chicken into a bowl.
5. In the same skillet, heat ½ tablespoon of oil on medium-high heat.
6. Add carrot, snow peas, apple and figs and stir fry for about 3 minutes.
7. Transfer the apple mixture into the bowl with chicken.
8. In the same skillet, heat remaining ½ tablespoon of oil on medium-high heat.
9. Add scallion and bok choy and stir fry for 1-2 minutes.
10. Add ½ cup of sauce and chicken mixture and bring a boil. Cook for about 2-3 minutes.
11. Serve hot.

Nutritional Information (Per Serving):
Calories: **325**
Fat: **10.8g**
Sat Fat: **1.8g**
Sodium: **550mg**
Carbohydrates: **38.2g**
Fiber: **6.5g**
Sugar: **26.7g**
Protein: **23.1g**

Chicken & Tofu Stir Fry

Servings: **6**
Preparation Time: **15minutes**
Cooking Time: **15 minutes**
Ingredients:
For Chicken Marinade:
- 1 medium scallion, chopped
- 3 tablespoons light soy sauce
- 3 tablespoons rice wine
- 1 tablespoon cornstarch
- 1 teaspoon white Sugar
- 2 (6-ounce) skinless, boneless chicken breasts, cut into bite sized pieces

For Stir Fry:
- 1 tablespoon olive oil
- 3 garlic cloves, minced
- 1 yellow onion, sliced thinly
- 1 green bell pepper, seeded and sliced thinly
- 1 red bell pepper, seeded and sliced thinly
- 12-ounce firm tofu, pressed and cubed
- 2 tablespoons oyster sauce
- ½ cup water

Direction
1. For chicken in a large bowl, mix together all ingredients except chicken.
2. Add chicken and coat with marinade generously.
3. Cover and refrigerate for about 30-40 minutes.
4. In a large skillet, heat oil on medium-high heat.

5. Add garlic and sauté for about 1 minute.
6. Add chicken with marinade and stir fry for about 4-5 minutes.
7. Add onion and bell peppers and stir fry for about 5 minutes.
8. Add remaining ingredients and cook for about 3-4 minutes.

Nutritional Information (Per Serving):
Calories: **175**
Fat: **6.9g**
Sat Fat: **1.6g**
Sodium: **485mg**
Carbohydrates: **12.4g**
Fiber: **1.8g**
Sugar: **6.2g**
Protein: **18.3g**

Chicken & Mixed Veggies Stir Fry

Servings: **6**
Preparation Time: **20 minutes**
Cooking Time: **17 minutes**
Ingredients:
For Chicken Marinade:
- 1 tablespoon garlic, minced
- 1 tablespoon fresh ginger, minced
- ¼ cup brown sugar
- 2/3 cup soy sauce
- 1 tablespoon cornstarch
- ¼ teaspoon red pepper flakes, crushed
- 3 (4-ounce) skinless, boneless chicken breasts, cut into thin strips

For Stir Fry:
- 2 tablespoons sesame oil, divided
- 1 onion, cut into chunks
- 1 (8-ounce) can water chestnuts, drained
- 1 green bell pepper, seeded and julienned
- 1 cup carrot, peeled and sliced thinly
- 1 head broccoli, cut into florets

Direction
1. For chicken in a large bowl, mix together all ingredients except chicken.
2. Add chicken and coat with marinade generously.
3. Cover and refrigerate for about 30-40 minutes.
4. In a large skillet, heat 1 tablespoon of oil on medium-high heat.

5. Add vegetables and stir fry for about 5 minutes.
6. Transfer vegetables in a large bowl. Cover with a foil paper to keep them warm.
7. In the same skillet, heat remaining oil on medium-high heat.
8. Remove chicken from bowl, reserving marinade.
9. Add chicken in the skillet and stir fry for about 4-5 minutes or till golden brown from all sides.
10. **Add cooked vegetables and reserved marinade and cook for 5-7 minutes.**

Nutritional Information (Per Serving):
Calories: **239**
Fat: **6.9g**
Sat Fat: **1.5g**
Sodium: **639**mg
Carbohydrates: **28.4g**
Fiber: **1.7g**
Sugar: **8.9g**
Protein:**16.0g**

Chicken, Mushrooms & Eggplant Stir Fry

Servings: **4**
Preparation Time: **20 minutes**
Cooking Time: **21 minutes**

Ingredients:
- ½ of large eggplant, cubed
- Salt, to taste
- 2 tablespoons canola oil, divided
- 2 garlic cloves, minced
- 4 (4-ounce) skinless, boneless chicken breasts, cubed
- 2 tablespoons soy sauce
- 2 cups fresh mushrooms, sliced
- 4 cups fresh spinach, torn
- Freshly ground black pepper, to taste

Directions:
1. In a bowl, place eggplant and sprinkle with some salt. Set aside for about 5 minutes.
2. In a large skillet, heat1 tablespoon of oil on medium heat.
3. Add garlic and sauté for about 1 minute.
4. Add chicken and stir fry for about 6-8 minutes.
5. Add soy sauce and stir fry for about 2 minutes more.
6. Add mushrooms and cook for 2-3 minutes.
7. Meanwhile in another skillet, heat remaining oil on medium heat.
8. Add eggplant and stir fry for about 3-4 minutes.

9. Add the cooked eggplant, spinach and black pepper in skillet with chicken.
10. **Stir fry for about 2-3 minutes or till spinach is wilted.**

Nutritional Information (Per Serving):
Calories: **239**
Fat: **11.4g**
Sat Fat: **2.1g**
Sodium: **557**mg
Carbohydrates: **6.7g**
Fiber: **3.1g**
Sugar: **2.6g**
Protein: **28.4g**

Chicken & Bok Choy Stir Fry With Almonds

Servings: **4**
Preparation Time: **20 minutes**
Cooking Time: **15 minutes**

Ingredients:
- 1 tablespoon cornstarch
- ¼ cup water
- 3 tablespoons peanut oil
- ½ cup whole almonds
- 1 (6-ounce) skinless, boneless chicken breasts, cut into thin strips
- ½ teaspoon ground ginger
- ¼ teaspoon garlic powder
- Salt and freshly ground black pepper, to taste
- 1 cup bok choy, chopped
- 1 cup mushrooms, sliced
- 1 cup celery, sliced
- 1 cup onion, sliced
- ¾ cup chicken broth

Directions:
1. In a bowl, mix together cornstarch and water. Keep aside.
2. In a large skillet, heat oil on medium high heat.
3. Add almonds and stir fry for about 2 minutes.
4. With a slotted spoon, transfer the almonds in a bowl. Keep aside.
5. In the same skillet, add chicken and stir fry for about 2-3 minutes.

6. Add ground ginger, garlic powder, salt and black pepper and stir fry for about 1 minute.
7. Add vegetables and stir fry for about 2 minutes.
8. Add chicken broth and reduce the heat to medium-low.
9. Cover and simmer for about 3 minutes.
10. Add cornstarch mixture, stirring continuously and cook for about 3-4 minutes.
11. **Top with almonds and serve.**

Nutritional Information (Per Serving):
Calories: **162**
Fat: **18.0**g
Sat Fat: **2.8g**
Sodium: **193**mg
Carbohydrates: **9.2g**
Fiber: **2.9g**
Sugar: **2.8g**
Protein: **14.3g**

Chicken & Carrot Stir Fry

Servings: **6**
Preparation Time: **20** minutes
Cooking Time: **13 minutes**

Ingredients:

For Sauce:
- 1 teaspoon fresh ginger, minced
- ¾ cup fresh orange juice
- 1 tablespoon cornstarch
- 1 tablespoon honey
- 3 tablespoons light soy sauce

For Stir Fry:
- 2 teaspoons peanut oil, divided
- 2 carrots, peeled and julienned
- 2 celery stalks, chopped
- 1½ pounds skinless, boneless chicken breasts, cut into thin strips
- ¼ cup scallion, chopped
- ¼ cup cashews

Directions:
1. In a bowl, mix together all sauce ingredients. Keep aside.
2. In a large skillet, heat 1 teaspoon of oil on medium-high heat.
3. Add carrot and celery and stir fry for about 3-4 minutes.
4. Add remaining oil and chicken and stir fry for about 5 minute.

5. Add sauce and stir fry for about 3-4 minutes.
6. Garnish with scallion and cashews and serve.

Nutritional Information (Per Serving):
Calories: **230**
Fat: **8.3g**
Sat Fat: **2.3g**
Sodium: **414**mg
Carbohydrates: **13.0g**
Fiber: **1.0g**
Sugar: **7.6g**
Protein: **27.0g**

Chicken & Apricot Stir Fry

Servings:**8**
Preparation Time: **15 minutes**
Cooking Time: **25 minutes**
Ingredients:
- 2 tablespoons olive oil
- 2 pounds skinless, boneless chicken breasts, cut into thin strips
- Salt and freshly ground black pepper, to taste
- 1 large onion, chopped
- ¼ cup balsamic vinegar
- 1 cup chicken broth
- 20 dried apricots, halved
- 1 cup apricot preserves
- ¼ cup fresh cilantro, chopped

Directions:
1. In a large skillet, heat oil on medium-high heat.
2. Add chicken and sprinkle with salt and black pepper and stir fry for about 5 minutes.
3. Add onion and stir fry for about 3 minutes.
4. Add vinegar and bring a simmer on medium heat. Cook for about 2 minutes.
5. Add broth and apricots and bring to a simmer.
6. Add apricot preserves and reduce the heat to medium-low.
7. Cover and simmer for about 10-15 minutes.
8. Serve with the garnishing of cilantro.

Nutritional Information (Per Serving):
Calories: **324**
Fat: **8.4**g
Sat Fat: **2.1g**
Sodium: **154**mg
Carbohydrates: **37.3g**
Fiber: **2.2g**
Sugar: **26.2g**
Protein: **27.6g**

Chicken, Bell Pepper & Pineapple Stir Fry

Servings: **4**
Preparation Time: **15 minutes**
Cooking Time: **25 minutes**

Ingredients:
- 1 tablespoon olive oil
- 1 large onion, cubed
- 1 teaspoon fresh ginger, minced
- 1 garlic clove, minced
- 2 (6-ounce) skinless, boneless chicken breasts, cubed
- 2 cups fresh pineapple, chopped
- 1 medium yellow bell pepper, seeded and chopped
- 1 medium red bell pepper, seeded and chopped
- 1 medium green bell pepper, seeded and chopped
- 2 tomatoes, seeded and chopped
- 2 tablespoons tamari
- 1 tablespoon apple cider vinegar
  - Salt and freshly ground pepper, to taste

Directions:

1. In a large skillet, heat oil on medium heat.
2. Add onion and stir fry for about 4-5 minutes.
3. Add ginger and garlic and stir fry for about 1minute.
4. Add chicken and cook for about 10 minutes.
5. Add pineapple, red bell peppers and tomatoes and cook for about 5-7 minutes.

6. Add tamari, vinegar, salt and pepper and cook for about 2-3 minutes more.

Nutritional Information (Per Serving):
Calories: **240**
Fat: **7.1g**
Sat Fat: **1.7g**
Sodium: **543**mg
Carbohydrates: **23.2g**
Fiber: **4.7g**
Sugar: **15.3g**
Protein: **22.3g**

Pork, Apple & Veggies Stir Fry

Servings: **4**
Preparation Time: **15 minutes**
Cooking Time: **18 minutes**

Ingredients:
- 1 tablespoon olive oil
- ½ pound lean minced pork
- 1 tablespoon ginger, minced
- 2 garlic cloves, minced
- 1 apple, cored and shredded
- 2 cups cabbage, shredded
- 1 large carrot, shredded
- ½ cup frozen peas, thawed
- 2 tablespoons soy sauce
- 1 tablespoon fish sauce
- Salt and freshly ground pepper, to taste
- 2 scallions, chopped

Directions:

1. In a large skillet, heat oil on medium heat.
2. Add pork and stir fry for about 4-5 minutes or till browned.
3. Add ginger and garlic and stir fry for about 1 minute.
4. Add apple and vegetables and stir fry for about 10 minutes.
5. Add soy sauce, fish sauce, salt and black pepper and cook for 1-2 minutes.
6. Garnish with scallion and serve.

Nutritional Information (Per Serving):
Calories: **101**
Fat: **3.8**g
Sat Fat: **0.6 g**
Sodium: **834**mg
Carbohydrates: **15.7g**
Fiber: **4.0g**
Sugar: **8.2g**
Protein: **2.8g**

Pork & Cucumbers Stir Fry

Servings: **4**
Preparation Time: **15 minutes**
Cooking Time: **10 minutes**

Ingredients:
- 3 tablespoon canola oil, divided
- 2 tablespoons fresh ginger, minced and divided
- 3 large cucumbers, peeled, seeded and cubed into ½-inch pieces
- 3 tablespoons soy sauce, divided
- ¼ cup scallion, chopped
- 2 garlic cloves, minced
- ½ teaspoon red pepper flakes, crushed
- 2 cups boneless pork, cut into bite sized pieces

Directions:
1. In a large skillet, heat 1 tablespoon of oil on high heat.
2. Add 1 tablespoon of ginger, cucumber and 1 tablespoon of soy sauce and stir fry for about 3-4 minutes.
3. Transfer the cucumber mixture in a large bowl. Cover with a foil to keep it warm.
4. In the same skillet, heat remaining oil on medium-high heat.
5. Add scallion, garlic and remaining ginger and stir fry for about 1 minute.
6. Add pork and stir fry for about 3 minutes.
7. Add remaining soy sauce and stir fry for 1-2 minutes more.

8. Serve pork with cucumber.

Nutritional Information (Per Serving):
Calories: **293**
Fat: **14.8g**
Sat Fat: **2.2g**
Sodium: **746mg**
Carbohydrates: **8.2g**
Fiber: **1.3g**
Sugar: **2.5g**
Protein: **31.7g**

Pork & Ginger Stir Fry

Servings:**2**
Preparation Time: **15 minutes**
Cooking Time: **15 minutes**
Ingredients:
- 2 tablespoons vegetable oil
- 1 teaspoon fresh ginger, sliced thinly
- ½ pound boneless pork, sliced thinly
- 2 teaspoons soy sauce
- ½ teaspoon sugar
- 1 tablespoon rice wine
- 1 teaspoon sesame oil
- Salt, to taste

Directions:
1. In a large skillet, heat oil on medium-high heat.
2. Add ginger and stir fry for about 1 minute.
3. Add pork and stir fry for about 5 minutes.
4. Add soy sauce and Sugar and stir fry for 5 minutes more.
5. Add remaining ingredients and stir fry for 3-4 minutes or till desired doneness.

Nutritional Information (Per Serving):
Calories: **325**
Fat: **19.9**g
Sat Fat: **4.4g**
Sodium: **506**mg
Carbohydrates: **5.5g**

Fiber: **0g**
Sugar: **3.1g**
Protein: **30.1g**

Pork, Snow Peas & Pineapple Stir Fry

Servings: **4**
Preparation Time: **15 minutes**
Cooking Time: **13 minutes**

Ingredients:
- 2 tablespoons vegetable oil
- 1 onion, sliced
- 1 garlic clove, minced
- ½ pound boneless pork loin, sliced thinly
- 1 cup snow peas, trimmed
- ½ cup fresh pineapple, cubed
- 1 fresh red chile pepper, seeded and chopped
- ¼ cup plum sauce

Directions:
1. In a large skillet, heat oil on medium-high heat.
2. Add onion and stir fry for about 4-5 minutes.
3. Add garlic and stir fry for about 1 minute.
4. Add pork and stir fry for about 2 minutes.
5. Add remaining ingredients and stir fry for about 4-5 minutes.

Nutritional Information (Per Serving):
Calories: **184**
Fat: **9.0g**
Sat Fat: **2.0g**
Sodium: **36mg**
Carbohydrates: **9.3g**
Fiber: **2.2g**

Sugar: **5.6g**
Protein: **16.7g**

Pork, Veggies & Peach Stir Fry

Servings: **4**
Preparation Time: **15 minutes**
Cooking Time: **25 minutes**
Ingredients:
For Pork Marinade:
- ¼ cup soy sauce
- ¼ cup fresh orange juice
- ½ teaspoon garlic powder
- ½ teaspoon ground ginger
- 1 pound boneless pork, cubed

For Stir Fry:
- 2 teaspoons sesame oil
- 1 large onion, chopped
- 1 cup small broccoli florets
- 1 large carrot, peeled and sliced thinly
- 1 (15-ounce) can sliced peaches (with juice)
- 1 tablespoon all-purpose flour

Directions:
1. For pork in a large bowl, mix together all ingredients except pork.
2. Add pork and coat with marinade generously.
3. Cover and refrigerate for about 6-8 hours.
4. In a large skillet, heat oil on medium-high heat.
5. Add onion and stir fry for about 4-5 minutes.
6. Add pork with marinade and stir fry for about 4-5 minutes.

7. Add broccoli and carrot and stir fry for about 2-3 minutes.
8. Add peaches with juice and bring to a boil. Slowly, add flour, stirring continuously for about 3-4 minutes or till sauce thickens.

Nutritional Information (Per Serving):
Calories: **278**
Fat: **6.7g**
Sat Fat: **1.7g**
Sodium: **985**mg
Carbohydrates: **21.6g**
Fiber: **3.7g**
Sugar: **13.5g**
Protein: **33.2g**

Garlicky Prawn Stir Fry

Servings: **4**
Preparation Time: **15 minutes**
Cooking Time: **7 minutes**
Ingredients:
- 1 tablespoon olive oil
- 3 garlic cloves, minced
- 1 pound prawns, deled and deveined
- 1 tablespoon honey
- 4 jalapeños, seeded and sliced
- ¼ cup fresh basil leaves, chopped
- Salt and freshly ground black pepper, to taste

Procedure:

1. In a large skillet, heat oil on medium heat.
2. Add garlic and stir fry for about 1 minute.
3. Add prawns and stir fry for about 3-4 minutes or till cooked through.
4. Add remaining ingredients and stir fry for about 2 minutes. Serve warm.

Nutritional Information (Per Serving):
Calories: **189**
Fat: **5.5g**
Sat Fat: **1.1g**
Sodium: **277mg**
Carbohydrates: **7.7g**
Fiber: **0g**

Sugar: **4.8g**
Protein: **26.2g**

Shrimp, Asparagus & Pasta Stir Fry

Servings: **2**
Preparation Time: **15 minutes**
Cooking Time: **7 minutes**
Ingredients:
For Sauce:
- ¼ cup chicken broth
- 1/3 cup mayonnaise
- 1 tablespoon fresh lemon juice
- 1 teaspoon fresh lemon rind, grated freshly

For Stir Fry:
- 1 teaspoon sesame oil
- 1 garlic clove, minced
- ½ tablespoon fresh ginger, minced
- ½ pound medium shrimp, peeled, deveined and halved
- ½ pound fresh asparagus, trimmed and cut into 1-inch pieces
- 1 cup cooked penne pasta

Directions:
1. For sauce in a large bowl, mix together all ingredients. Keep aside.
5. In a large skillet, heat oil on medium heat.
6. Add garlic and ginger and stir fry for about 1 minute.
2. Add shrimp and asparagus s and stir fry for about 3 minutes.
3. Add cooked pasta and sauce and stir fry for about 3 minutes.

Nutritional Information (Per Serving):
Calories: **502**
Fat: **18.6**g
Sat Fat: **2.6g**
Sodium: **652**mg
Carbohydrates: **50.7g**
Fiber: **2.7g**
Sugar: **5.0g**
Protein: **35.3g**

www.ingramcontent.com/pod-product-compliance
Lightning Source LLC
Chambersburg PA
CBHW071441070526
44578CB00001B/180